Baby Boomers' Legacy and Last Chance

Are We Leaving Enough
for Other Generations?

*To book store manager, Guy.
Hope you enjoy the book.
Best wishes,*

George Hanuschak Sr.

George Hanuschak Sr.

The front cover represents the roles of the Baby Boomer Generation and the roles of Generation X and Generation Y (or millennials). The baby robins in the nest represent Generation X and the millennials, who need the love and support of the Baby Boomer Generation (the fully grown robins). The Baby Boomer Generation needs to supply the food and nutrients to the baby birds, just like the Greatest Generation and the Silent Generation did for the Baby Boomer Generation. The cover is symbolic of the relationship among these five generations.

ISBN 978-0-578-17909-4

Printed in the United States of America
Signature Book Printing, www.sbpbooks.com

Table of Contents

Acknowledgments

I especially want to thank my immediate family members for their wonderful love and support throughout the writing period. They include my wonderful and supportive wife, Regina, and our two sons, John and George Jr. Sadly, my mother Flora and my sister Jean passed away during this period. They were able to read a draft of the book and comment on it based upon their experiences. I want to dedicate this book to my wife and two sons, my deceased mother and sister, and my deceased father Mickey. He was a member of the Greatest Generation and served 4 years in the U.S. Navy during World War II, first as a gunner's mate and then mostly as a signalman. He traversed over 125,000 nautical miles while serving on four different ships. I also want to dedicate the book to two of my closest high school friends, John and Frankie, who were both killed in action in the Vietnam War. My talented wife edited the book and improved the readability considerably. My son George Jr. designed the book covers. My son John made several suggestions. A former co-worker and long-time friend, Mike Craig, also edited the book. Another former co-worker and friend, Peter Gajary, helped form some of the ideas for the book with numerous lunch discussions and some early research. Another former co-worker and friend, Sonia Hickman, helped me with the information technology aspects of publishing the book.

Beth Rosenfeld did the significant reformatting to prepare the book for printing. Her patience with a new author was especially appreciated. Anne Mattison did the final copy edit. Signature Book Printing helped with the final print preparations and in finishing the book cover design.

Preface

My intent for this book was quite simple. It was to describe the experiences and the legacy of the United States of America's Baby Boomer Generation. The book begins with a tribute to the Greatest Generation, which is described in Tom Brokaw's book *The Greatest Generation* and elsewhere. The Greatest Generation, those born from 1901–1924, and the Silent Generation, those born from 1925–1945, faced two almost unbelievable challenges, the Great Depression starting in 1929 and then World War II from 1941–1945. After the war, families began to have more children; those children born between 1946 and 1964 are referred to as the Baby Boomer Generation. There were 79 million baby boomers. This book attempts to describe some of the experiences, impressive accomplishments and legacies, and a few negative characteristics, of this generation. The author is a baby boomer, but the book is not autobiographical in nature; it is mostly based on research of existing information about the Baby Boomer Generation. Some of the author's personal experiences and opinions may be reflected but are kept to a minimum. The book ends with a description of the current and future federal debt challenge and some potential longer-term solutions as described by the Simpson-Bowles Commission and others, including some with different approaches. The potential solutions will involve considerable sacrifices by some members of all six of the current living generations, mostly those who are financially able to contribute to the complex and demanding solutions. The United States still has the greatest research and development infrastructure in the world, which will definitely aid in the process of finding even more potential solutions. The energy outlook is quite bright, with domestic oil and natural gas production increasing, and future growth in green energies should help the economy grow faster again. Of course the Great Recession of 2007–2009 took a major toll on the economy, including the loss of millions of jobs. Over the past several years, we have had a very slow but very steady reduction in unemployment, which is currently below 5 percent. Some remaining concerns include stagnant wages for many, reduction in full-time employment and benefit options, shrinking of the middle class as a result of manufacturing declines, and some severe differences in the economy geographically. The author feels that the United States, however, will be able over the next several decades to meet the very tough challenge of taking care of an aging Baby Boomer Generation, while providing great opportunities for Generation X and Generation Y members, the latter of which are known as millennials. Generation X, Y and Z members are the children and grandchildren of the baby boomers. The baby boomers, like their Greatest Generation and Silent Generation parents, want to provide excellent opportunities for their children and grandchildren.

About the Author

After graduating from high school in Ohio, the author graduated from Youngstown State University in Ohio in 1971 with a bachelor's degree in mathematics. He then obtained a graduate teaching associate position at Ohio State University and graduated in 1973 with a master's degree in mathematical statistics. In 1980-1981 the federal government sponsored him to attend Cornell University to study graduate-level public management. He completed a 1-year academic program called Education for Public Management.

In his post-graduate career, the author joined the U.S. Department of Agriculture's (USDA) National Agricultural Statistics Service (NASS) as a mathematical statistician in 1973. He worked for the agency for 34 years as a mathematical statistician, a supervisory mathematical statistician and finally as a member of the Senior Executive Service. For most of his career, the author was involved in statistical research aimed at improving the methodology and accuracy of the nation's agricultural statistics. His specialty became the use of earth observation satellite data to develop crop area mapping and perform crop area estimation. Such maps and estimates are still being produced by USDA NASS today. During his career, the author published more than 30 research papers on improving agricultural statistics.

The author also helped other nations around the world improve their agricultural statistics programs. He worked with the governments of Costa Rica, France, Jamaica and Morocco; the European Union; and the United Nations Food and Agriculture organization.

The author is a member of the Baby Boomer Generation, which is the topic of this book.

Chapter I
The Legacy of the Greatest Generation

Tom Brokaw did a superb job of writing his book *The Greatest Generation*. The Greatest Generation, consisting of those born from 1901–1924, is well-known for its incredible sacrifices for the United States and the world. The greatest of these were seen in surviving the Great Depression (1929–1930s) and in the phenomenal sacrifices made and bravery demonstrated in World War II. The war resulted in the death of 406,000 American soldiers and the wounding of more than 600,000. More than 16 million Americans served bravely in this massive war. They saved the world from the cruel dictatorship of Adolph Hitler and the threat of Japanese invasion, as demonstrated in the Pearl Harbor attack. Mr. Brokaw outlined the lives and experiences of specific members of the Greatest Generation in his book to illustrate this. Some experiences were so painful that many never wanted to speak about them ever again; many did not speak about them until decades later. The one example that stands out among many was the experience of the soldiers on the beaches at Normandy, where thousands were killed on D-Day. It took a powerful alliance of the United States, the United Kingdom, France, Russia and

1

other allies to succeed. More than 50 million people died worldwide in World War II. Very difficult decisions had to be made by pre–Greatest Generation Presidents Franklin D. Roosevelt and Harry S. Truman.

Mr. Brokaw, on the back cover of his book, describes members of the Greatest Generation in glowing terms: "They came of age during the Great Depression and the Second World War and went on to build modern America—men and women whose everyday lives of duty, honor, achievement, and courage gave us the world we have today."[1]

Members of this generation also picked themselves up by their bootstraps during and after the Great Depression. Levels of unemployment and underemployment were the highest in the nation's history for nearly a decade. Yet somehow, most of the people persevered through great economic sacrifice. They needed to stand in massive soup lines to survive. Two and three generations had to live together in small apartments and small homes, sometimes with heating hard to come by in very cold areas of the country.

---

[1] Brokaw, Tom. *The Greatest Generation*. Random House. 1998.

Things were booming in the early 1920s before the massive stock market crash of 1929. One terrible memory was the suicides on Wall Street as some failing investors jumped from buildings to their deaths below. Many Greatest Generation members were children or teenagers at the time. The impact on their psyches was severe since they had to help their parents and families survive such devastating economic blows.

Two major federal efforts from this era were designed to help in the slow and often painful recovery. The first was the establishment of The Banking Act of 1933, which created the Federal Deposit Insurance Corporation (FDIC). Congress and President Franklin D. Roosevelt established the FDIC to protect the bank accounts of depositors, preventing future runs on banks. The FDIC, which is still in place, has helped in the current bank-related crisis and helped during the Great Recession of 2007–2009. The second major federal effort was the Social Security program, created in 1935. In 1940, the program had fewer than 250,000 beneficiaries; now there are over 50 million. The importance of these efforts led by President Roosevelt and Congress cannot be overstated: They helped members of the Greatest Generation and are helping their baby boomer children decades later.

A third but smaller program was the establishment of the Civilian Conservation Corps. From 1933–1943, over 2.5 million young men worked in this program to help support themselves and their struggling families. They received room and board and a $30 monthly payment, $25 of which they had to send back home to their parents. During this period, over 3 billion trees were planted in a major reforestation effort. It was not until the massive war buildup that the economy got a full boost to recover from the Great Depression. War supplies the nation needed, including the famous Liberty ships, had to be produced at an unprecedented pace. Eighteen American shipyards built 2,710 Liberty cargo ships from 1941–1945. This was by far the largest number of ships ever built to one design.

These terrible experiences drove the Silent Generation (also known as the Traditionalist Generation) and Greatest Generation members to provide their baby boomer children with much better opportunities, especially economically and educationally. Baby boomer children were told repeatedly by their parents, "If you can't afford it, don't get it." An exception was made for a small mortgage, if one could afford a down payment and had prospective income to eventually pay off the mortgage (and the sooner the better.) The education level of many

Greatest Generation members was limited because of the unaffordable cost of higher education. One obstacle to affordable education was removed by passage of the 1944 GI Bill of Rights, which helped millions of military personnel obtain formal education after the war. Seeing the value of that educational opportunity drove Greatest Generation members to make higher education a very high priority for their children.

Another extremely positive characteristic of the Silent Generation and Greatest Generation was the impressive teamwork and camaraderie that members of these generations developed while facing great challenges. During World War II, soldiers from all parts of American society had to work together to accomplish their great missions. One exception was that African-American soldiers were maintained in segregated units. Yet despite this treatment, these soldiers were high performing and highly motivated. For example, the Tuskegee airmen of the U.S. Army Air Force, who were detailed in the recent movie "Red Tails," participated in many heroic efforts. Another exception was the Navajo Indian Code Talkers, who used their native language for critical secret wartime communications. The Germans never were able to break the Navajo code. Service members in general though were very much appreciated by American society after returning from a war that was publicly supported from beginning to end. Major parades and celebrations took place in the streets of New York City and in many other cities around the country.

Unfortunately, this generation faced a third significant challenge by having to fight in the Korean War. One personality that stood out to the author was the Hall of Fame baseball player Ted Williams. He fought in World War II and the Korean War as a U.S. Marine Corps fighter pilot. He flew 39 missions in the Korean War, and between the two wars he lost nearly 5 years of his Hall of Fame baseball career. He simply felt that it was his patriotic duty to serve. Military units were also being racially integrated to comply with President Truman's executive order in 1948 to begin troop integration.

The demilitarized zone between North and South Korea remains today, and tensions are high again with North Korea's threat of nuclear weapon use. This remains a serious concern for South Korea, Japan, China and the United States at a minimum. Hopefully, a peaceful solution can and will be reached with multiple talks and enforceable agreements among nations. As expressed in his book, Tom Brokaw believes the world owes the Greatest Generation incredible gratitude.

The Silent Generation had some of the same attributes and experiences as the Greatest Generation and generally will be considered together for this book. The earliest members of the Silent Generation were just a few years old when the Great Depression hit. Some of the earliest members also served in World War II and later members in the Korean War.

One of the more famous members of the Greatest Generation was President John F. Kennedy. Civil rights leader Dr. Martin Luther King Jr. and Senator Robert F. Kennedy were members of the Silent Generation. Sadly, all three leaders were assassinated in the prime of their lives.

Rosa Parks, a Greatest Generation member, stood out with her very brave civil rights stance on a bus in the South in 1955.

Most of the famous leaders during the Great Depression and World War II were members of the pre–Greatest Generation, such as President Franklin D. Roosevelt, President Harry S. Truman and General Dwight D. Eisenhower, who later became president. However, they depended on the millions of American men and women

7

from the Greatest Generation and Silent Generation to carry out their policies during these crisis periods.

Chapter II
Baby Boomers' Youth and Early Adulthood

The Baby Boomer Generation in the United States is generally defined as consisting of those born between 1946 and 1964. It includes 79 million persons. This book addresses both the experiences and impacts of this generation on society, including the great, the good and sometimes the bad. Members of this generation have faced experiences much different from their Greatest Generation parents. Many of their parents were part of an immigration boom early in the 20th century. From 1900–1920, there were 14.5 million immigrants, mostly from Europe. Many of them were processed at Ellis Island in the New York City area. Their children, and children not from immigrant families, became the Greatest Generation. At the end of World War II, when Greatest Generation military members returned from war, they began to have children, later referred to as the Baby Boomer Generation because of their large numbers.

The boomers' youth was spent primarily in the 1950s, the 1960s, and for the youngest of the baby boomers, the 1970s. The 1950s was one of the most stable periods in American history. The Greatest Generation general,

Dwight D. Eisenhower, was president from 1952–1960. This era included a growing and stable economy with a very strong manufacturing base, including the steel, automotive and textile industries at or approaching a peak. President Eisenhower and Congress initiated funding for the vast American highway system to be built. Many other industries were also doing very well, including chemical, energy, transportation, tourism and entertainment. Unemployment and inflation were relatively low during this period. The middle class and blue collar workforce of the Greatest Generation made economic and quality-of-life strides for themselves and their baby boomer children. Members of this workforce emphasized home ownership and saving for their baby boomer children's college education.

Strong family values were even reflected in famous television shows like "Leave It to Beaver" and "Ozzie and Harriet." The value of education was often drilled into the young baby boomers by their parents. In many cases, all family members were expected to start saving for a child's college education as soon as possible. Child-rearing books by Dr. Benjamin Spock and others encouraged a gentler, kinder method of child rearing and strongly discouraged any form of physical discipline. But some believed that the gentler, kinder pendulum may have swung too far. Baby boomers were often labeled as the "me generation" and may have taken many good things for granted.

During the 1960s, civil rights tensions continued to grow as the large economic gap between minorities and Caucasians increased. Thus, prospects were pretty good for a young Beaver Cleaver but not necessarily for many minority children. This discrepancy was also reflected in television programs. Another decade went by before African-American–based programs finally appeared, such as "Sanford and Son" (which began in 1972) and "Good Times" (which began in 1974). In 1975 a Hispanic-based program called "Popi" began, with Hector Elizondo cast as the main character. The series "Good Times" (which began in 1974) reflected strong family values by people living in a poor inner city housing project.

Thousands of playgrounds and recreational facilities were built for baby boomer children to enjoy. From the inner cities to the expanding suburbs to rural areas, children had many opportunities to enjoy such facilities. Many included basketball courts, tennis courts, baseball fields, swimming pools, swings and play centers with slides. Children often spent hours at such facilities, and many went to them daily. The opportunity to play and get involved in sports helped children in their physical and social development. Crime rates were generally much lower than they are now, and children were generally very safe at such facilities with minimal parental supervision. Many baby boomer children experienced very pleasant childhoods.

When not at school or at playgrounds, children found quality books to read. Some of these were inherited from the Greatest Generation, and families even discussed and shared their joy of particular books. Child drama and fantasy series like the Hardy Boys and Nancy Drew were very popular. Another source of education and entertainment was television. Television shows included those already mentioned plus "Lassie," "Zorro" and "Popeye the Sailor." Cowboy movies were also a big hit. Davy Crockett raccoon skin caps, including the raccoon tail, and Barbie dolls were well-liked. If the baby boomer children just did well in school and were generally well-behaved, their parents were quite happy with them.

The 1960s brought very different experiences, some positive and some tragic, and influences on the still young and impressionable Baby Boomer Generation. Some of the major events that impacted them were the election of John F. Kennedy as president, his public assassination in

1963, the Civil Rights Act of 1964, the Voting Rights Act of 1965, the assassinations of Dr. Martin Luther King Jr. and Robert Kennedy in 1968, the Vietnam War and the Woodstock music festival. Strong educational opportunities remained as many baby boomers went to college in the mid- to late 1960s, although the number of opportunities remained lower for minorities. The 1960s saw the breakout of famous singing groups like Elvis Presley, the Beatles and many Motown stars. The 1960s saw the National Aeronautics and Space Administration (NASA) send astronauts to walk on the moon. As the baby boomers were being college educated, they were exposed to and began to participate in more social and political changes. This was quite different from the relatively calm childhood of the early baby boomers in the 1950s.

Later baby boomers, those born between 1958 and 1964, did not experience the calmness of the 1950s, and more of their childhood was spent in the 1960s and even in the 1970s. Some of their memories might include events such as the end of the Vietnam War, President Nixon's resignation, his pardon by President Gerald Ford, the shooting deaths of four college students at Kent State University in 1970, the Iran hostage crisis and the failed helicopter rescue attempt, the waiting lines for gasoline during the oil crisis, and the massive volcanic eruption of Mount

Saint Helens. Other memories might include the death of Elvis Presley, the assassination of John Lennon, the beginning of MTV and CNN, the movie "E.T.," the first "Star Wars" movie, the release of the Pac-Man video game, Sally Ride as the first female astronaut, television shows like "MASH" and "Miami Vice" and the building of the Vietnam Memorial.

On the sports front, these boomers likely remember the mega-fights between Mohammed Ali and Joe Frazier; the rivalry in golf among Arnold Palmer, Jack Nicklaus and Gary Player; and the emergence of Tiger Woods. In basketball, there were the multiple national titles won by the Boston Celtics, Los Angeles Lakers, Chicago Bulls and Detroit Pistons and by UCLA, Duke and North Carolina. Boomers also likely remember the tennis matches between Jimmy Connors and Bjorn Borg and between Chris Evert and Martina Navratilova as well as the U.S. hockey team upset of the Russian team in the Olympics. The sports industry and other famous athletes are covered later in the book.

On the economic front, strong growth continued for many industries throughout the baby boomer period. Industries such as the steel, rubber, chemical, pharmaceutical, automobile, trucking, energy, tourism, music and entertainment, sports, art and museum, television, transportation, space, real estate, financial and retail industries expanded throughout and often well beyond the 1960s. Many of these industries will be further elaborated on later in this book, citing their growth periods and, in some cases, their decline.

Chapter III
Baby Boomers' Early Experiences and Legacies

One of the great accomplishments of the Baby Boomer Generation, initiated by their parents, was civil rights advocacy for women and African-Americans. At times it was a very rocky road. During the Greatest Generation, there was the famous Rosa Parks incident in 1955, where Ms. Parks was told to sit at the back of a public bus just because she was African-American; she bravely refused. It took several more tragedies to awaken more Americans to civil rights violations. Some of the tragedies included the bombing in 1963 of an African-American church, in Birmingham, Alabama, where four African-American girls were killed; the assassination of Medgar Evers in 1963 in Mississippi; the cruel police actions in Selma, Alabama; and the murder of four civil rights workers in Mississippi in 1964. Some of these tragedies were covered on national television and awakened many more Americans to civil rights violations.

The National Association for the Advancement of Colored People (NAACP), the Southern Christian Leadership Conference, Dr. Martin Luther King Jr. and other civil rights leaders peacefully protested against such unjust and tragic acts. Dr. King eloquently discussed the many great struggles in his famous "I Have a Dream" speech on the National Mall in Washington, D.C., in 1963, after which policies and situations began to improve. Dr. King believed that integration and nonviolence were the necessary tools of progress, based partially on Mahatma Gandhi's efforts in India in the 1940s. The political and social alliance of the John F. Kennedy administration and Dr. King became a powerful force for improvement.

After the shocking assassination of President Kennedy in 1963, President Lyndon Johnson followed up on many of the civil rights dreams of the Kennedy administration by pursuing new civil rights legislation, getting it approved by Congress and signing it into law. Dr. King received the Nobel Peace Prize at age 35, the youngest person ever to be granted this world-recognized award. Then in 1968, the nation endured two more assassinations: Dr. King in April 1968 in Memphis, Tennessee, and Robert F. Kennedy in June 1968 in Los Angeles. These three assassinations, of President Kennedy, Dr. King and Robert F. Kennedy, took a major psychological toll on many baby boomers.

Unfortunately, in the mid- to late 1960s, things temporarily turned more violent with major racially based riots in New York City, Los Angeles, Chicago, Cleveland, Detroit, Washington and other cities. After much destruction in some of the inner city neighborhoods of these cities and even some deaths, things eventually began to calm down.

The great melting pot of ethnicity, sex and eventually race is one of the United States' great accomplishments. Uniting millions of people who once bore more of an "us versus them" mentality was truly important for a more complete democracy. It was especially difficult and painful for African-Americans and women, who were denied many basic rights for far too long. Amazingly, it was a president from the South, Lyndon Johnson, who was able to implement many of the civil rights dreams of President John F. Kennedy. The Civil Rights Act of 1964, the Voting Rights Act of 1965, the beginning of new social programs (such as Medicare and Medicaid) for nearly all elderly Americans and the growth of employment opportunities for minorities and women all contributed to the inclusive melting pot accomplishment. Of course women's right to vote came during the Greatest Generation after the women's suffrage protests and efforts. During the baby boomer period, the use of upward mobility programs and other vehicles such as affirmative action enhanced opportunities for many minorities and women. To this day, not all is perfect, especially for those in poverty-stricken inner city communities, but the United States is a much more inclusive society than it was 50 years ago. It was a very difficult journey, but the results have been critical to the improvement of society for all.

Drug use was an extremely negative development for the Baby Boomer Generation. This development began with the hippie and anti-war subculture and expanded over time. The first widespread television exposure was anti-war demonstrations and the infamous 1969 Woodstock festival in New York state. Over 500,000 participants showed up for a 4-day music festival on a small 600-acre dairy farm. Some participants used marijuana, LSD, opium, cocaine, psychedelic mushrooms and alcohol. These negative aspects dominated television media coverage, but there were also thousands of peaceful participants just enjoying the music. However, the coverage of drug use and sometimes public sex gave much of the television audience a very negative view. It also didn't help when headline performers Jimmy Hendrix and Janice Joplin died of drug overdoses a year later. In addition, many soldiers in Vietnam were exposed to drugs. In any event, considerable drug use continued among some of the Baby Boomer Generation for decades.

The demand for drugs in the United States grew, and society also paid another dear price with crime rates in the United States steadily rising during the decades of the Baby Boomer Generation. These are aggregate trends and are not meant to imply that all or nearly all baby boomers participated in these activities. In 1960, 288,000 violent crimes were committed in the United States, which had a total population of 179 million. By 1980, more than 1.3 million violent crimes were committed, when the population was 225 million. Baby boomers ranged from age 16 to age 34 in 1980. Interestingly enough, the crime rate dropped some during the Great Recession of 2007–2009. This at first puzzled some criminologists, but after further study they found some reasons for this phenomenon. A leading criminologist at Northeastern University in Boston, James Alan Fox, and some colleagues list four major reasons: Baby boomers were middle-aged or older, computers and geographic information systems were used as police aids, more incarcerations took place and sentences were longer, and the crack cocaine epidemic, which peaked from 1984 until 1990, was waning. One most unfortunate ramification of a new crime law in 1994 was mandatory sentencing for first-time drug users, even those caught with small amounts. This led to the over-incarceration of millions of youth, especially young African-Americans. In retrospect, the law should have focused almost entirely on major drug dealers. The law was in most respects a success in reducing crime but came at too large a price for one group of Americans. The legacy of much higher drug use and crime rates during the Baby Boomer Generation compared with previous U.S. generations is certainly a negative one. The Baby Boomer Generation has been labeled the "me generation" for some of its self-indulgences. The drug legacy cannot be erased, but baby boomers can discourage the use of drugs by their children and grandchildren and inform them about the terrible individual and societal costs.

Currently there is a widespread epidemic of methamphetamine and heroin use, especially in the Midwest and New England. Heroin overdose deaths have tripled during the past decade. Silent Generation, Baby Boomer Generation and Generation X politicians, social workers and parents are leading a movement to educate the public on the effects and treatment of illegal drug use. The demand and supply of illegal drugs nationally and globally must also be reduced.

The epidemics of obesity and diabetes began to develop during the Baby Boomer Generation. (The author has no formal medical training so will only make general observations or mention those from reputable medical sources such as the American Medical Association and the Centers for Disease Control and Prevention [CDC].) The fast food industry grew exponentially in the 1950s, 1960s and 1970s. Millions of baby boomers began to eat at fast food restaurants. The food tasted very good, was served quickly and was priced reasonably. For example, McDonald's now has over 1.8 million employees and over 33,000 locations worldwide. Many baby boomers loved the convenience, often having short lunch periods while at work. Their children also came to love the food. Unfortunately, this great-tasting food and the soft drinks served with it were often high in saturated fat, sugar and salt. CDC recently published a study covering the years 1995–2010, which shows that the rate of diabetes more than doubled in the United States during this time. In some states, the increase was more than 150 percent. Another downside of fast food is that high blood pressure often results from excessive salt intake, which often occurs with fast food consumption. Besides the rapid growth in fast food consumption, well-advertised sugary cereals became very popular, especially with children. In

1920, sugar consumption averaged 65 pounds of sugar per person per year. In 2000, the average was about 100 pounds per person per year. In 2012, the average was approximately 155 pounds per person per year. Medical professionals consider the epidemic of type II diabetes to be related to this high sugar consumption. These trends are serious and add substantially to aggregate health care costs.

On the bright side, better nutrition information and health education is reaching many baby boomers and their children. The popular television show "The Dr. Oz Show"; the recent book by Joel Fuhrman, *Eat to Live*; and the emphasis on a healthier lifestyle by Michelle Obama and others are beginning to affect more people. Many baby boomers have joined gyms or health spas or participate in fitness classes such as Zumba. In fairness to the fast food industry, many fast food restaurants are offering healthier options, such as salads, fish and fruit smoothies. Even so, nutrition education for the masses will need to reach a higher percentage of the population. Lowering the rates of obesity, type II diabetes and high blood pressure is key to lowering health care costs, but this may take decades. Consumers, after all, still have freedom of choice to eat and drink what they want in a free and democratic society.

There were many bright spots and developments during the Baby Boomer Generation as well. Obviously, millions upon millions of baby boomers did not become drug addicts or criminals. Many baby boomers, with their advanced levels of education, became outstanding scientists, business professionals, doctors, professors, teachers, etc. In addition, numerous medical breakthroughs and new drugs helped baby boomers and their ailing parents. Millions of Americans are being treated with effective drugs for numerous conditions, including diabetes, heart conditions, cancer, high blood pressure, high cholesterol, anxiety, depression and attention deficit disorder. Though drugs' side effects are sometimes serious, in aggregate, millions of Americans have benefited immensely from them

On the economic side, the U.S. auto, steel, rubber and other manufacturing industries were booming during the Baby Boomer Generation, with many middle class jobs created as a result. (The decline of some of these industries will be covered later in the book.) Jobs were created for nurses, plumbers, electricians, home construction workers, teachers, police officers, firefighters, medical technicians, textile workers, chemical and energy-related workers, economists, statisticians, engineers, etc.

The music industry was booming as well. Famous Motown stars, such as the Temptations, the Supremes, Smokey Robinson and the Miracles and Sam Cooke, as well as non-Motown superstars such as Elvis Presley and the Beatles, were formed during the baby boomer years and became incredibly popular with young baby boomers. Other stars included Barbara Streisand, Andy Williams, Roberta Flack, Aretha Franklin, Celine Dion, Jackie Wilson, Linda Ronstadt, the Everly Brothers, Creedence Clearwater Revival, Chicago, Bob Dylan, Johnny Cash, Dolly Parton, the Beach Boys, Whitney Houston and thousands more. Some of these entertainers were pre–baby boomers born around 1940, and many were baby boomers born after 1945. Most of the audiences consisted of baby boomers. The quality of the music from this golden period is still recognized today.

Tense relations between the United States and Russia from 1945–1991, termed the Cold War, began at the Yalta Conference in 1945. President Truman and Russian Prime Minister Joseph Stalin completely disagreed on how to handle postwar Germany. The United States, ignoring Russian opposition, established the Marshall Plan, which aided in the reconstruction of West Germany. The United States–backed International Monetary Fund and World Bank helped stabilize war-torn Europe.

Russia occupied East Germany and all of Eastern Europe behind the Iron Curtain, with a wall dividing East and West Germany. Both the United States and Russia expanded their nuclear weapon and conventional warfare capabilities during this period of very tense relations.

It was not until the Cuban Missile Crisis in 1962 that major policy changes were evaluated and implemented over time. The U.S. Central Intelligence Agency (CIA) was reported to have failed at (1) several assassination attempts of Fidel Castro, the Communist leader of Cuba, and (2) the Bay of Pigs planned invasion of Cuba. This infuriated Castro, who turned to Russia for help. The resulting Russian nuclear warheads placed in Cuba, so close to the U.S. mainland, brought the world to the brink of nuclear war. Fortunately, after a U.S. Navy blockade and showdown, the leaders of Russia and the United States were able, at seemingly the last minute, to avert this calamity for the world.

Nuclear control talks began in the 1970s. The first Strategic Arms Limitation Talks (SALT I) led to an agreement in 1972, and SALT II brought further progress in 1979. The United States did not ratify the SALT II treaty because Russia chose to invade Afghanistan, and Russia and the United States continued to spar. President

Reagan challenged Russian Prime Minister Mikhail Gorbachev concerning the Berlin Wall in a speech in which he demanded, "Mr. Gorbachev, tear down this wall." Prime Minister Gorbachev, progressive in comparison to his predecessors, declared in his book *Perestroika: New Thinking for Our Country and the World*, "We are all passengers aboard one ship, the Earth, and we must not allow it to be wrecked. There will be no second Noah's Ark."[2]

Eventually, the Eastern Bloc countries were able to free themselves from Russian control, the Berlin Wall was torn down and a new era began.

The Baby Boomer Generation's strong support for reductions in nuclear arms and long-range anti-ballistic missiles was key to a successful resolution. Continued talks in the 1990s between the United States and Russia, which led to the Strategic Arms Reduction Treaties (START I and START II), resulted in further reductions in nuclear arsenals and therefore a safer world. Current talks on continued nuclear war arsenal reductions are taking

---

[2] Gorbachev, Mikhail. *Perestroika: New Thinking for Our Country and the World*. Harper & Row Publishers. 1987.

place between the two nations. Currently, North Korea and Iran are creating major nuclear arsenal concerns.

In the mid- to late 1960s and even the early 1970s, the Baby Boomer Generation faced perhaps its greatest challenge, the Vietnam War. Over time, it resulted in the first major clash among members of the Baby Boomer Generation. As with most wars, it started with strong national support. Some members of the Baby Boomer Generation back home in the United States began to challenge the policies of the war and publicly protested against it. In the midst of such demonstrations at home, hundreds of thousands of baby boomer soldiers served bravely in Vietnam. The death toll was approximately 58,000, and the wounded toll was in the hundreds of thousands. The Vietnam War was the first war covered on live television, and the ugliness of war was exposed to millions back home. In war, a handful of troops may succumb to severe stress and snap. Unfortunately, this was the case in the My Lai Massacre of an entire village by U.S. troops. It must be remembered as an aberration; the vast majority of the hundreds of thousands troops served valiantly in a difficult war. The troops were not responsible for the policies and attempted to carry out their mission as prescribed by the administration and military leaders.

Unfortunately, when the troops began to return home, they faced a lack of acceptance by some of their own Baby Boomer Generation members. This was an especially hurtful experience for these veterans. The protests continued to grow, and a terrible event in 1970 occurred at Kent State University in Ohio: Four war-protesting students were gunned down and killed by members of the Ohio National Guard. As a result, more than 500 colleges were temporarily shut down to avoid any further violence. Due to increasing public pressure, the Vietnam War was ended in 1972 by President Richard Nixon. It was a painful chapter all around for the Baby Boomer Generation. Several movies about the Vietnam experience were produced and shown about 20 years after the war. One of these, "Born on the Fourth of July," starring Tom Cruise, revealed the raw emotions from all sides of the controversial and painful issues.

In the mid-1970s, a new economic crisis began in the United States. The oil shortage began when the Organization of Petroleum Exporting Countries (OPEC) decided to curtail production. Oil prices surged as the United States relied on imports for much of its oil supply, and shortages of gasoline led to long lines at U.S. gas stations. Gasoline rationing was implemented based on license plate numbers. The term "misery index" was used to describe the simultaneous very high inflation rates and interest rates. It was a wake-up call about how dependent the United States had become on oil imports from sources that were not always reliable. Early attempts at alternative energy sources were tried but generally were not yet ready for cost-effective mass utilization.

Back to the topic of education, the 1944 GI Bill enabled many of the later members of the Greatest Generation to advance their education after World War II. From 1944–1956, it enabled 2.3 million to attend college and 6.6 million to finish high school, go to trade school or get on-the-job training. The veterans valued these opportunities because many of their peers had to curtail their schooling due to the Great Depression and World War II.

Hence, one of the most important and major goals of the Greatest Generation and Silent Generation became providing their baby boomer children with a level of formal education greater than their own. This major dream was fully realized due to their guidance and economic sacrifice for their children. The percentage of Baby Boomer Generation who attended high school and went on to higher education more than doubled in comparison with their parents. It was a source of great pride for Greatest Generation parents to speak of their children's educational accomplishments. As a result of the advanced level of education and a healthy and growing economy, many baby boomers had exceptional career opportunities. GI Bills continue to this day to help veterans obtain more education after their military service.

The following graph on educational attainment comes from the U.S. Department of Education. It shows steady growth and a great education success story from the GI Bill to current times. Millions of baby boomers, Generation Xers, and millennials have received bachelor's degrees. This fact alone would make many Great and Silent Generation members proud.

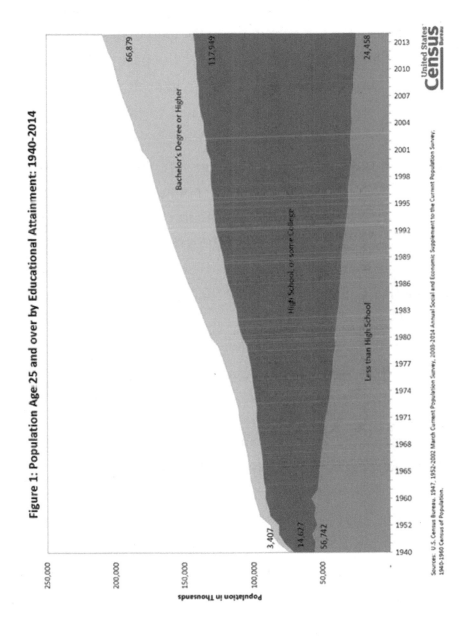

Figure 1: Population Age 25 and over by Educational Attainment: 1940-2014

A more recent unfortunate trend is that many college graduates have a substantial college loan debt to pay off. Student loan debt has doubled over the past decade and is now about $1.3 trillion in aggregate. It has become harder for many to find a job related to their education because of the 2007–2009 Great Recession, so some are unemployed and many are underemployed. Some of them have had to move back home with their baby boomer parents. Baby boomers with children to support and elderly parents to help at the same time are now labeled as members of the "Sandwich Generation." This group is feeling some serious economic stress. One recent bright spot is that federal data shows a 63 percent increase in the amount of master's degrees granted by U.S. universities and colleges from 2000–2012, despite rising costs for students and their families in some cases.

Another serious and unfortunate development has been the disappearance of many middle class jobs and a drop in real income since around 2000. The gap between the well-off and the middle class and the poor has been growing rapidly. If this gap becomes too large, it could lead to societal unrest. Even with the very substantial social programs by federal, state and local governments (such as Social Security, Medicare, Medicaid and extended unemployment insurance), the gap is still growing.

The Food Stamp Program (now called the Supplemental Nutrition Assistance Program [SNAP]) alone grew dramatically during the baby boomer period and has nearly doubled since the 2007–2009 Great Recession. In 1966, there were only 1 million recipients; in 2012, the number jumped to an astounding 48 million. Also, the jobs being created during the slow recovery are often lower paying than the jobs lost. The U.S. Bureau of Labor Statistics estimates that a net 5 million manufacturing jobs were lost from 2000–2016. There has been a recent uptick in manufacturing jobs since 2010. Since January 2010, about 800,000 manufacturing jobs were created.

The total number of manufacturing jobs is currently 12.3 million compared with a peak of around 19.5 million in the mid- to late 1970s and a low of 11.5 million in early 2010. However, the number of U.S. services jobs was around 66 million in 1980 and is now around 120 million. This data shows a major transition in the U.S. economy from manufacturing to services.

An interesting political observation is that baby boomers were largely responsible for the election of presidents from both the Republican and Democratic parties. Let's assume that Presidents Eisenhower and Kennedy were largely elected by the baby boomers' parents. The 1968 election had a large influx of baby boomers voting for president for the first time. In 1968, both the baby boomers and their parents elected Richard M. Nixon as president. After Nixon resigned, Vice President Gerald Ford was declared president. Subsequently, the baby boomers voted in every presidential election from Jimmy Carter to Barack Obama. One of the goals of this author is to stay bipartisan and not to defend or deny any party their moments of representation in the White House and the Congress. The only observation is that baby boomers voted for both parties over time to occupy the presidency and the House of Representatives and the Senate.

On the subject of women's rights, President John F. Kennedy established the Presidential Commission on the Status of Women, with Eleanor Roosevelt as chair. The commission's report found many injustices against women and suggested corrective actions. Women's voting rights had been long established by the suffrage movement in the 1920s. In 1963, Betty Friedan published her book, *The Feminine Mystique*, which became a best seller and launched a renewed women's rights effort. In 1963, Congress passed the Equal Pay Act. In 1964, President Lyndon Johnson signed the Civil Rights Act, giving African-Americans and women additional freedoms and rights. The act also created the Equal Employment Opportunity Commission (EEOC) to investigate complaints and impose penalties for violators. In 1966, the National Organization for Women (NOW) was established. In 1965 and 1967, President Johnson established affirmative action policies for minorities and woman. These policies were effective for decades but came under court case challenges; in 2003, the Supreme Court ruled, in two cases, to uphold affirmative action but with more restrictions on direct point systems used in college admissions.

Other landmark Supreme Court decisions affected the Baby Boomer Generation. In *Brown v. Board of Education*, in 1954, the court ruled that "separate but equal" public facilities had no place in the United States. The decision remained controversial for a decade until the Civil Rights Act of 1964 made racial equality a matter of federal law. In another controversial decision, in 1962, the Supreme Court ruled public-school–sponsored prayer unconstitutional. In 1966, the *Miranda v. Arizona* decision established the principle that criminal suspects must be advised of their rights before being interrogated. In 1973, the very controversial *Roe v. Wade* decision legalized abortion. In 1974, the Supreme Court ruled against President Richard Nixon's plea to keep the Watergate tapes private. President Nixon resigned just 2 weeks after the Supreme Court ruling.

The baby boomers picked up and extended the women's rights movement during their decades of influence. There are now increasing percentages of women in Congress, state and local governments, high-level business positions (such as CEOs) and graduate schools, including medical and law schools.

Chapter IV
Review of Computer, Internet and Cell Phone Industries

The phenomenal growth in the use of personal computers by baby boomers and their children and grandchildren has led to impressive gains in productivity. The first personal computers were designed by late-member Greatest Generation scientists and businessmen and then advanced by baby boomers. Personal computers have been used in business and at home by millions of new users. From 1975–2011, personal computer sales in the United States grew from 40,000 units to 95 million units. In the same period, worldwide sales grew from 50,000 units to 355 million units. Companies also successfully developed necessary peripherals, like laser and ink jet printers, modems and, more recently, wireless communication devices. Computer development and usage has been an incredible growth industry for the United States, with companies like Microsoft, Intel, Apple, Oracle, Dell, IBM, HP and Xerox being developed or enhanced around the mass utilization of personal and business computers and peripherals.

Some rather incredible baby boomers like Bill Gates, Steve Jobs, Larry Ellison, Michael Dell, Michael Bloomberg and others have benefited financially from this rapid deployment and utilization of personal and business computers. Even before the personal computer revolution, there was a very strong business mainframe and mini-computer industry, with companies like IBM, DEC, Xerox and others involved. This development improved many processes and increased productivity in many U.S. businesses. There was also a smaller but important development of a supercomputer industry, first dominated by Cray Computer Company (Seymour Cray developed the Cray supercomputers). Large science labs, universities and large businesses use these computers to solve very intensive number-crunching applications. In fact, the use of these supercomputers has grown recently, even during the slow recovery from the Great Recession of 2007–2009. The National Science Foundation (NSF) is currently partially funding new supercomputers for several major research labs, such as the National Center for Supercomputing Applications at the University of Illinois at Urbana-Champaign. Some of the most recent developments for personal use are laptops, tablet computers and smart cell phones, which are reaching baby boomers and their children and grandchildren.

The Internet was initially developed by the U.S. military and large university research labs with the Department of Defense's Advanced Research Projects Agency Network (ARPANET). Email for authorized users was first available there for a decade or so. Then there was an explosion of new, commercial Internet-based companies such as Amazon, Google, eBay and AOL that were quite successful and grew rapidly. The linkage of computers by powerful networks enhanced computer use even more. In the mid- to late 1990s, the NASDAQ technology stock index rose from 600 in 1996 to 5,000 in 2000. In the late 1990s, there was fallout from the dot.com boom and a major reduction in value and size for some companies. The NASDAQ fell from 5,000 to 2,000 and eventually to 800 in 2002. Some companies (like Apple, Amazon and Google) have survived with the aid of new products or improved software. The successes of Apple under Steve Jobs, Microsoft under Bill Gates, and Amazon under Jeff Bezos are well-known.

Another phenomenal development has been the cell phone. It is now 40 years old and was developed by late-member Greatest Generation or Silent Generation scientists. The first handheld units were quite large and heavy by today's standards. From 1990–2011, worldwide use of cell phones has experienced unbelievable growth, from

12.4 million units to 6 *billion* units! The vast majority of baby boomers, their children and even some grandchildren have cell phones. Thus the creation and use of cell phones has crossed at least four generations to date. Some powerhouse companies in this industry are Apple and Samsung for hardware and AT&T, Verizon, T-Mobile and Sprint for service providers. Add the development of today's social media tools (Facebook, YouTube, Skype, Twitter and others) to this growth. These developments have helped families across the world and across generations to effectively communicate in new fashions. Facebook founder and CEO Mark Zuckerberg is a member of Generation Y (those born between 1981–2000). Interestingly, Bill Gates, Steve Jobs and Mark Zuckerberg never graduated from college and are poster children for the American Dream.

The growth of the television industry was phenomenal during the Baby Boomer Generation. As children, many baby boomers started with black and white medium-resolution televisions with just a few channels available. Many baby boomers can remember the first time they saw a television program in color. Now, the average family has multiple high-resolution color televisions with either cable or satellite dish service; the service is often combined with high-speed Internet access and, more recently, "bundled" with home phone service.

Chapter V
Housing and Banking Developments

The U.S. banking industry has a long and generally successful history for its members and their millions of clients, at least since the Great Depression and the adoption and creation of the FDIC. It is tempting to remember only the negative periods of U.S. banking, such as the Great Depression, the Great Recession of 2007–2009 and the savings and loan crisis of the late 1980s. However, the banking industry has successfully served the American public for decades with savings and checking accounts, certificates of deposits (CDs), money market accounts, mortgage and home improvement loans, automobile loans, education loans, re-financing of mortgage loans and so forth. It is a very essential industry for a capitalistic and democratic society. A relatively healthy credit union industry also remains and did generally well even from 2007–2010. Credit unions tend to be smaller and more regional or with a specific clientele (e.g., the Navy Federal Credit Union). Some believe that an increase in the number of regional and smaller banks and credit unions would be better for consumers than being stuck with using the top 5 to 10 superbanks. There will likely always be debate on how to regulate this industry.

The rest of this section will briefly attempt to cover banking's difficult periods. In the late 1970s, interest rates were quite high for those able to save. CDs and savings accounts were paying high interest rates. However, in 1980 the savings and loan associations (S&Ls) were deregulated, giving them bank-like capabilities but without many of the banks' regulations and protections. The deregulation eventually led to the S&L crisis of the late 1980s. William Seidman, former chair of the FDIC and the Resolution Trust Corporation (RTC) stated, "The S&L banking problems of the 1980s and 1990s came primarily, but not exclusively, from unsound real estate lending." Mortgage loans grew from 700 billion in 1976 to 1.2 trillion in 1980. Interest rates on CDs were very high before the crisis hit. As part of the solution, in 1989, Congress passed the Financial Institutions Reform, Recovery and Enforcement Act, which established the Savings Association Insurance Fund (SAIF) and gave it to the FDIC. In addition, the Office of Thrift Supervision (OTS) was established to charter, regulate, examine and supervise savings institutions.

U.S. home ownership jumped for both the Greatest Generation and the baby boomers from 1945–2004. The home ownership rate in 1940, before the war, was 44 percent. By 1960, it had risen to 64 percent. Then, as baby boomers became of home-ownership age, home ownership peaked at 69 percent in 2004. Many baby boomers with good middle class jobs were able to purchase homes from 1980 until the 2004 peak. In addition, there was a rapid rise in home prices, and homes with larger square footage became more popular. There was a sudden real estate boom in many communities where housing values increased rapidly, providing great investment opportunities for owners and landlords. Many owners and landlords increased their wealth several fold, especially during the 1990s. Many baby boomers took out home equity loans to finance some of their children's college expenses and some home improvements and to pay off family health care costs and so forth.

The credit card industry began as a consumer aid in flexible financing. However, over time, some consumers ran up credit card debt balances, including interest and in some cases penalties. Some of this debt was reduced during the Great Recession of 2007–2009, but the total in aggregate remains around $1 trillion. Credit cards and now debit cards remain handy tools for consumer flexibility as long as individuals don't get into serious debt trouble.

Some felt the housing bubble of the 1990s and early 2000s would never burst, but it eventually did. Mortgage loans were granted too freely to prospective clients, with tools like balloon payments and no interest payments in the first 10 years of a loan. Speculation in housing and real estate ran rampant until, in 2007, it became apparent the country was on the verge of a financial collapse. Some major banks had mortgage loan debts beyond their cash reserves. Some newer tools, like collateralized debt obligations and credit default swaps, seemed to accelerate problems. By October 2008, U.S. Treasury Secretary Hank Paulson and President George W. Bush became convinced that a major government intervention was needed to prevent a potential collapse of the U.S. finance industry. The Bush administration's first act was the Emergency Economic Stabilization Act, followed by the Troubled Asset Relief Program (TARP), with congressional approval.

After the election of Barack Obama in 2008, TARP was initiated and expanded. General Motors and Chrysler Corporation needed government bailouts, as well as Fannie Mae and Freddie Mac. There was great debate about the need for intervention, the level of intervention and the types of intervention required. (The author is not a banking analyst or professional economist, so these observations are based on reported expert opinions.) Most economists say unemployment would have been even higher without intervention, but the debate continues for some to this date. The Dodd-Frank Act of 2010 is still being implemented and has strong proponents and strong detractors. There is also a new worldwide banking regulation, Basil III, being implemented as well.

By 2012 the home ownership rate had dropped to 65 percent. The Great Recession (2007–2009), lax lending practices and rampant speculation all contributed to the decline. Housing values dropped significantly, and the number of foreclosures and distress sales grew significantly. A small but still delicate rebound began in late 2012 and 2013. Hopefully, it will proceed at a reasonable rate of growth; the continued very low interest rates and the pent up demand from Generation X buyers are somewhat promising.

I realize that my brief attempt at summarizing this crisis is perhaps oversimplified. We must continue to strive for the best regulatory environment in which to provide financial services to the U.S. public, with the least amount of missteps for all concerned. A capitalistic system is dependent on a well-run financial system. It will likely remain a large private sector enterprise, with strong federal regulation necessary as well. A 2013 special section by Jonathan Rosenthal in *The Economist* did an excellent job of summarizing the current and potential future status of the U.S. and world banking industries from a more technical and professional perspective.

The U.S. stock market has outperformed most other types of investments over long periods. Of course, any particular stock can and sometimes does lose money. The stock market has been reasonably strong over the past year or so. However, when the Federal Reserve changes its monetary policy of incredibly low interest rates, it is likely to adversely affect the market unless U.S. economic growth increases more rapidly. A substantial increase in interest rates can also dramatically increase the federal debt. However, it will help savers and others. The issue of interest rates set by the Federal Reserve is quite complex.

Chapter VI
Terrorism and Natural Disasters

No American can forget the tragic terrorism inflicted on the United States on September 11, 2001. The Twin Towers in New York City were brought down by terrorists flying commercial airliners. Similar crashes occurred at the Pentagon and in a farm field in Pennsylvania. These four terrorist-hijacked plane crashes ultimately cost the lives of thousands of innocent U.S. citizens. The bravery of the first responders will also never be forgotten by the American public. The images are burned in our memories, and our thoughts and prayers are still with the victims (including many first responders) and their extended families. The United States had to defend itself against Usama Bin Laden and his group of terrorists who were responsible for the attacks. Bin Laden was able to avoid capture for 10 years, but in 2011 he was located and killed by a U.S. Navy Seals team in Pakistan.

The terrorist attacks also seriously affected the U.S. economy, with a drop in the stock market (the Dow Jones index fell from 11,700 to 7,300) and a surge in federal spending for security enhancements and the war in Iraq and then Afghanistan. As a result of these great sacrifices by baby boomers and their children, a new post 9/11 GI Bill was passed, giving some returning veterans educational opportunities. Many of these very brave American soldiers served in multiple tours under very dangerous conditions.

In a 1995 domestic act of terrorism, a very disturbed U.S. citizen bombed a federal building in Oklahoma City. The bombing killed 168 people, including young children in a day care center in the building. In 2013, another terrible domestic bombing occurred at the Boston Marathon.

Most unfortunately, there has been an outbreak of public shootings in schools and other public places. In a number of these horrific and heinous acts, schoolchildren were killed. Mass shootings occurred at Columbine High School in Colorado; at a school in Jonesboro, Arkansas; at Virginia Tech University; and at Sandy Hook Elementary School in Newtown, Connecticut. Other shootings occurred in a mall and a movie theatre in Colorado, at Fort Hood, and in the Washington, D.C., area. There have been other similar incidents over the past several years.

Six mass shootings in the past year have stunned the nation. A shooting in an Orlando, Florida, LGBT nightclub by an ISIS supporter who hated LGBT people killed 49 people. The shooter's motivation is still under FBI investigation. A racially motivated shooting took place in a church in Charleston, South Carolina. Shootings also occurred in San Bernardino, California; Colorado Springs, Colorado; Roseburg, Oregon; and Chattanooga, Tennessee. All these tragic incidents involved some form of hatred and/or terrorism and/or mental illness and access to rapid-fire guns. All these shootings left 89 people dead and numerous people seriously injured. There is no one cause or one solution. Therefore, the question for American society is: Is there a combination of partial solutions that can at least reduce the probability of such tragic events in the future?

Policy-makers are currently struggling to find ways to reduce the likelihood of future shootings. The partial solutions likely will involve some combination of policies and programs: improved methods for detecting and treating mental illness; some form of stricter gun control; less use of hate speech, especially by leaders in society; stricter monitoring of potential terrorists; stricter parental guidance for children's video games and extremely violent movies; and improvement and expansion of security, especially for soft targets.

The Baby Boomer Generation has also experienced its share of natural disasters. Both the East Coast and the Gulf Coast are prone to major hurricanes. Many of these disasters are etched in our memories since there was wide and frequent television coverage. The first such disaster probably remembered by most baby boomers was a Category 5 hurricane named Camille that hit Louisiana and Mississippi and caused major flooding in Virginia in 1969. In 1989, Hurricane Hugo, a Category 4, hit South Carolina, causing some deaths and major property damage. The most expensive of the recent hurricanes was Hurricane Andrew, a Category 5 that hit Homestead, Florida, in 1992 and was almost a direct hit on Miami. Many lives were lost, and the economic toll was about $26.5 billion. Hurricane Ike hit Cuba, Haiti and the United States in 2008. As for other major U.S. disasters, the volcanic eruption of Mount St. Helens was previously mentioned, and the country's floods, forest fires, mudslides, sinkholes and droughts are too many to list.

The Midwest is especially prone to tornados. On April 3, 1974, there was the largest tornado outbreak in U.S. history, affecting both populated and rural areas. In one day there were 148 tornados reported in 13 states, 30 of which were the most violent types known (F4 and F5 on the Fujita scale). There were over 300 fatalities and over 5,500 injuries. Weather radar at the time could show and predict severe storms but not tornados, so there were no warnings.

The 1974 tragedy led to a significant research and development effort by the federal government and private sector to improve weather forecasting systems, especially for tornados. As a result, a weather warning system via radio was developed and implemented in the late 1970s. In the mid-1990s, a high-resolution system called Doppler radar was implemented, and tornado warnings were dramatically improved. It is estimated that an outbreak today like the 1974 one would have about a third of the fatalities. In fact, a large outbreak occurred in 2008 with 87 fatalities reported. Also in 2008, super-high resolution was added to the National Weather Service (NWS) warning system; dual polarization was added in 2012. In 1974, the average baby boomer was around 19 years old. These advanced weather warning systems were first built by the Great and Silent Generations and then improved by the baby boomers. Tornado warnings can now be issued about 16 minutes *before* a tornado hits, saving many lives and demonstrating the power of the combination of the three generations.

The images of the 2004 Indian Ocean tsunami and the 2011 Japanese tsunami are also burned into our national psyche. One of Mother Nature's most violent forms, the tsunamis caused many fatalities and truly tragic suffering among many people. After an earthquake greater than 9.0 on the Richter scale launched the massive Indian Ocean tsunami, the death toll was over 230,000. Indonesia, Sri Lanka, India and Thailand all suffered fatalities and massive property damage. Also created by an earthquake, the 2011 tsunami in Japan caused over 20,000 deaths and serious nuclear plant damage and radiation leakage. The United States did provide substantial aid in both of these horrendous cases, as well as for Haiti after its 2010 earthquake.

Another weather-related disaster occurred in the New Orleans area with 2005's Hurricane Katrina and its major flooding in the city and Gulf Coast areas. Some of the federal, state and local government responses seemed quite inadequate at times as many citizens suffered immense losses of life, limbs and property. Some citizens were never able to return to New Orleans. Communities such as Houston, Texas, and church groups throughout the country took some of these people in and helped them rebuild their lives. When General Russel Honoré took over the federal military relief, the response efforts improved substantially. The federal government eventually spent a large sum to reinforce the water control system for New Orleans.

A 2010 tragic fire and explosion at the Deepwater Horizon drilling station caused a massive oil leak directly into the Gulf of Mexico's waters and coastal wetlands and tributaries. The explosion killed 11 crew members and innumerable fish and birds. Several attempts were made to stop the leak before it was finally capped. Eventually British Petroleum (BP) agreed to refund some of the losses (over $25 billion so far).

In 2012, the hurricane and northeaster Superstorm Sandy struck much of the eastern U.S. coast. Sandy killed approximately 150 people and caused incredible property damage, extended loss of power, severe beach erosion and flooding from New Jersey to New England. There was even some wind damage and loss of power as far south as Maryland, Washington, D.C., and Virginia.

U.S. citizens generally respond well during major disasters to help their fellow citizens and people around the world. Aid is not always implemented perfectly by federal, state and local governments but is usually quite substantial nevertheless. These levels of government have significant resources and staff to help in such emergencies.

It is important to remember that, in spite of all these horrendous acts of terrorism and terrible natural disasters, the American spirit remains high. Although it was somewhat anguishing to write about these disasters, it is a tribute to all Americans that we still strongly believe in our open and democratic society. All five generations— the Greatest Generation, Silent Generation, Baby Boomer Generation, Generation X and Generation Y—have retained their strength in the face of adversity. After all, Americans also enjoy simple, daily joys such as weddings; the births of children, grandchildren and even great grandchildren; and watching one's children develop through all aspects of a productive life. Every day, Americans working in the public and private sectors are providing valuable products and services to their fellow citizens. In the author's opinion, the United States remains the best nation in the history of the world, and it is a privilege to be an American citizen.

Chapter VII
Accomplishments in Space, Industry and the Arts

Space

Established by President Eisenhower and strongly supported by President Kennedy, the U.S. space program has been a marvelous, multi-generational national accomplishment. The Russian Sputnik launch in 1957 sparked the United States' desire to enter the space race and develop an entirely new program and industry. This effort was led by Greatest Generation and Silent Generation scientists and astronauts and then expanded by Baby Boomer Generation scientists and astronauts such as Alan Sheppard, Neil Armstrong, John Glenn, Gus Grissom, Deke Slayton and Sally Ride. The space program has had many direct benefits: Earth observation, planetary telescoping, communications satellites, weather satellites and exploration of the moon, Mars, the sun and beyond. An incredible amount of new knowledge has been accumulated about the Earth and the entire planetary system.

Of course, the two fatal manned-spacecraft accidents were part of a high human sacrifice in the mission attempts. Their tragic images are also emblazoned in the United States' psyche. Those brave astronauts gave their lives to advance the world's knowledge of space. Currently, the International Space Station remains active, and some relatively new public–private partnerships are underway. In addition, the National Oceanic and Atmospheric Administration (NOAA) has steadily improved weather observation satellites, leading to more accurate warnings for hurricanes, tornados, floods and severe storms.

Among the many space mission spinoffs, one was the development of geospatial technologies such as Global Positioning System (GPS) technology, which can be used to fight diseases and crime and create interactive maps for everyday use. NASA and NOAA have excellent websites detailing the thousands of space program spinoffs: Improved suits and equipment for first responders; miniature heart pumps; light-emitting diodes for cancer tumor detection and treatment; robotics; long-distance health care procedures; improved crop estimation and mapping and forecasting procedures used by the U.S. Department of Agriculture (USDA); and lightweight materials for many applications.

A 2013 public television show, "Earth from Space," showed some of the truly amazing natural processes discovered from observation satellites developed in the past 10 years. Among those is the source of the oceans' salt. There is a massive waterfall of very intense salt brine under the Antarctic ice that guides the ocean currents and temperatures. Another is the fertilization of the Amazon by dust storms from the Sahara desert; the storms carry fertilizer from ancient lake bottoms across the southern Atlantic Ocean and deposit it in the Amazon.

Thousands of highly educated and motivated baby boomers were involved in the space program and its spinoffs. It is estimated that the space program has created over 1,300 new technologies.

Agriculture

The U.S. agricultural economy has had various degrees of success, but it is very strong at the moment and likely to remain so for the foreseeable future. The USDA and land-grant university agricultural research programs have led to some phenomenal successes over the Greatest Generation and baby boomer decades. This system produced government and university research and development, as well as a strong system for transferring new methods to farmers. The father of the green revolution of crops was Dr. Norman Borlaug, a Greatest Generation scientist. It is estimated that his methods of improving crop yields saved millions of lives around the world. In 1970, he was awarded the Nobel Peace Prize and, in 1977, the U.S. Presidential Medal of Freedom. His methods were carried out by thousands of baby boomer scientists in the 1970s and beyond.

U.S. agriculture has experienced down cycles as well. For example, in late 1998, hog prices fell drastically, and producers were endangered. Prices fell to less than a third of the preceding year's average. The slaughterhouses helped set a floor to the prices, stopping the steep decline. Although farmland prices have varied quite a bit over several decades, they are currently quite high and stable. The crop yield green revolution, crop varieties, livestock weight gains per unit of input and many other advances are due to the use of new and improved methods and products by thousands of Greatest Generation and baby boomer researchers, farmers, agri-business employees and retail food sector employees.

The United States has been truly blessed with over 300 million acres of cropland for corn, soybeans, wheat, cotton, rice, fruits, nuts and vegetables. Most of this acreage is rain-fed on good soils and with proper climate. This places the United States in a very strong position. Humans' two most basic needs are food and potable water, even before shelter and clothing, which means the outlook should remain bright for the U.S. agricultural economy. In fact, it has been quite strong even during the Great Recession of 2007–2009. According to data published by the U.S. Department of Agriculture's National Agricultural Statistics Service, cropland values rose more than 15 percent from 2006–2009. In 2015, cropland values were reported at $4,000 per acre.

Several of the new products in demand have been ethanol and biofuels. Although a severe drought in 2012 reduced crop yields and stressed livestock herds (in aggregate due to subsidized federal crop insurance and very high prices for those who had crops to sell), the U.S. agricultural economy remains quite strong in a historic sense. This may change some as non-food plants such as grasses and weeds from river buffers and other non-crop lands are used when economically feasible for ethanol and biofuel production. At that point, there may be a drop in some demand for corn and some other crops, but the worldwide demand for food should remain strong due to increasing consumption in China, India and other countries.

There was a large increase in cigarette and tobacco usage during World War I and considerably more growth in World War II. When these soldiers returned from war, they continued smoking cigarettes. Of course, there was no widespread indication of potential health issues during those times. Cigarette consumption remained high during the Vietnam War and now included hundreds of thousands of baby boomers. However, back home, information about health related risks was beginning to surface. The 1964 U.S. Surgeon General's report, "Smoking and Health," increased public awareness of potential risks, such as throat and lung cancer. Over the next 3 or 4 decades, the baby boomers dramatically reduced their cigarette consumption.

Chemical Industry

The U.S. chemical industry has been very strong throughout the entire baby boomer period. The United States is currently the leading nation for chemical production and products. About 80 percent of the output is polymer and plastic related. Another major product is gasoline refined for cars and trucks. Some major companies in the industry are Exxon Mobil, Chevron, Dow Chemical, DuPont, Lyondell/Basell and PPG. There are still thousands of good jobs remaining in this industry, including those for the middle class.

The chemical industry delivers very essential products to the U.S. economy and citizens, usually without negative incidents. However, people still remember the industry's major accident in Bhopal, India, in 1984. A Union Carbide plant leaked a massive toxic cloud that killed 6,000 people immediately and eventually over 20,000 total. Another major negative event was the tragic toxic dumping and cover-up in New York State by an obsolete company in 1953. A small number of executives decided to secretly dump very toxic chemicals (mostly benzene) at their site in the Niagara Falls area. They then sold the property to the city for $1. City officials unwittingly allowed the property to be developed into a small housing complex, which included an elementary school. People began to get very sick, and there were birth defects and other terrible health consequences such as leukemia. This became known as the Love Canal environmental disaster. Even in the Greatest Generation and Silent Generation, there were a few corrupt and greedy individuals. The Love Canal caused public outrage and eventually led to many congressional acts: The Toxic Substances Control Act, the Clean Water Act, the Clean Air Act, the Pesticide Act, the Safe Drinking Water Act and the Resource Conservation and Recovery Act. The Love Canal and other potentially dangerous industry-caused situations led to stronger oversight of industries by the Environmental Protection Agency (EPA) and state agencies.

There is a rather delicate balance between regulation and valuable and economic industry products that is always the subject of debate. Some very important industries (such as chemical and energy) do have some risks to society, but they have many benefits as well. There has to be certain oversight but also not stifling regulations. The current balance, although not perfect, keeps the very important chemical industry quite strong in both Western Europe and the United States.

Retail Industry

The growth of the U.S. retail sales industry during the baby boomer decades has been rather phenomenal, since boomers have been the United States' and the world's biggest consumers for decades now. The stories of Sears, J.C. Penney, Kmart, Walmart, Target and many others are incredible. Walmart alone employs over 2 million people, as many as the U.S. federal civilian workforce. The baby boomer middle class grew because of industries like steel, rubber, automobiles, airline travel, tourism, agriculture, clothing and textiles. The industries' continual and often rapid development created a mass of baby boomer workers and consumers. U.S. imports grew as boomers' powerful demand encouraged international companies to send products to the United States, such as Japanese automobiles, French wine, Italian and other ethnic foods and manufactured products from China, India and other countries.

Travel and Tourism

During the baby boomer period, there has also been incredible growth in the travel and tourism industries. The National Highway System, started under President Eisenhower in the 1950s, has expanded dramatically since its inception. Every region of the country eventually received long east–west and north–south highways. Millions have used the system for family vacations and tourism, including "snowbirds": Midwesterners and Northeasterners who travel to Florida for a few weeks or months each year to avoid winter. This phenomenon has sparked the massive growth of Florida's tourism economy. Coastal beaches were Florida's most popular destinations until the opening of Walt Disney World in 1971 and other large amusement parks in Orlando. On the West Coast, California saw a similar phenomenon even earlier, as Disneyland was established in 1955. With the advent of affordable commercial air travel, Hawaii developed a very large and successful tourism industry. There are also many regional amusement parks, such as Six Flags and Cedar Point. Skiers travel to snowy areas like Colorado and Utah during winter.

Mass Transit

The oldest mass transit and first metro transportation systems in the United States were developed by the Greatest Generation's parents and the Greatest Generation. The oldest systems are in Boston and New York City and are over 100 years old; Chicago's "L" system started in 1921. Most of the expansion and updating of these three systems have been carried out by the baby boomers. There are at least two other large systems that, although initially planned by Greatest Generation members, were mostly expanded during the baby boomer period: San Francisco's Bay Area Rapid Transit (BART) and the Washington, D.C., Metro system. BART opened in 1972 and is still being expanded. D.C.'s Metro system opened in 1976 and is also undergoing expansion, even as current safety risks are being addressed. Millions of commuters use these mass transit systems every day, a fact that was highlighted in 2003, when the East Coast electric grid failed and over a million New York City commuters had to walk home across some of the city's major bridges. It was a very impressive display of positive human interaction and support, as there were virtually no crimes or panicking by the huge crowd. However, major maintenance and modernization (including improvements in cybersecurity) is overdue for much of the U.S. infrastructure, such as roads, highways, bridges, electrical grids and energy pipelines and storage.

Pharmaceutical Industry

The pharmaceutical industry has been expanding greatly for over 50 years. It has developed many new and highly effective medicines for high blood pressure, diabetes, heart disease, cancer, stroke, mental health and other serious illnesses. The drugs have successfully been used by millions of Americans and others. Thousands of baby boomers were involved in this development. Vaccines for diseases such as polio, hepatitis, measles, scabies and the flu, along with very powerful, effective antibiotics, have been developed and used by millions of Americans. Of course, there is also a price to society, with the medicines' potential for side effects and even death, but overall, millions more are helped than hurt. It is the responsibility of the Food and Drug Administration (FDA) to evaluate medicines for their public safety and to recall them, if necessary.

There is concern that "superbugs" are becoming resistant to the antibiotics currently available. The United States uses about 40 million pounds of antibiotics every year for human health and for livestock production. Again, over-all, many more lives have been saved by these new med-icines over the past 5 decades or so. Even the more con-troversial alternative medicines, most of which have not been tested by clinical trials, help some people reduce negative health symptoms.

Another recent health concern is the Zika virus, which is spread by mosquitos and is especially dangerous for childbearing women because this is no cure yet.

Human Genome and Brain Mapping

One of the Baby Boomer Generation's major scientific ac-complishments was the mapping of the Human Genome, which took 13 years of excellent research. The project was led by two top-notch baby boomer scientists, Aristi-des Patrinos, Department of Energy, and Francis Collins, National Institutes of Health. The United States led the effort, which also involved international scientists and organizations. The project's findings were a real boost to the biotechnology industry and also led to some very important medical developments, such as genetic markers for some major diseases. Francis Collins is now the director of the National Institutes of Health and directly involved in the new proposal for human brain mapping, which will probably lead to some impressive breakthroughs over the next decade.

As the baby boomers age, a serious future health concern is the expected increase in persons diagnosed with Alzheimer's. It is a tragic disease not only for the patient but also for the caretakers and other family members and friends. The financial costs of Alzheimer's to families and to Medicare and Medicaid are also expected to increase. The Human Genome Project and the new brain mapping initiative will shed light on the disease, but real progress will probably take several decades.

The use of nanotechnology, sometimes combined with other technologies such as robotics, has recently shown great promise for medical applications, including better cancer cell detection and monitoring, even of individual brain tumor cells. Researchers say that not all brain tumor or other types of cancer cells are equal. Portions of a tumor that contain super-aggressive cells may be able to be identified and treated accordingly. These developments are not a cure for cancer but can improve cancer identification and treatment.

To put nanotechnology into perspective, a nanometer is one-billionth of a meter. The average human cell measures about 10,000 nanometers. The potential for addressing individual cells in the human body seems mindboggling. Nanotechnology is still in its infancy, but its potential in medicine alone is astounding. Several other medical applications for nanotechnology also look promising, such as using for it for performing eye surgery and identifying heart attack warning signs.

Sports

Like the generations before them, U.S. baby boomers really love their sports. American football, basketball, boxing, hockey, golf, auto racing and baseball are world class. Baby boomers heard stories from their parents about the likes of Babe Ruth, Lou Gehrig, Joe DiMaggio, Joe Louis, Gordie Howe, Bobby Orr, Babe Didrickson Zaharias, Mickey Wright and hundreds of others. As both professional and amateur sports programs have expanded greatly, famous sports heroes who entertained, and some who continue to entertain, the Baby Boomer Generation and who were not mentioned earlier in the book have emerged: Bill Russell, Wilt Chamberlain, Serena Williams, Jack Nicklaus, Rocky Marciano, Sugar Ray Robinson, Ben Hogan, Bobby Jones, Wayne Gretsky, Jim Brown, Gale Sayers, Hank Aaron, Michael Jordan, Magic Johnson, Larry Bird, Rod Hover, Mickey Mantle, Willie Mays, Sandy Koufax, Nancy Lopez, Roberto Clemente, Alex Rodriguez, Steffi Graf, Tamika Catchings, Kareem Abdul-Jabbar, Dale Earnhardt, Mario Andretti, Dale Earnhardt Jr., Richard Petty, Walter Payton and coaches Vince Lombardi (of Green Bay Packers fame) and John Wooden (of the UCLA basketball dynasty) are among the hundreds of Hall of Fame athletes and coaches. Each baby boomer sports fan probably has his or her own list of the top 100 and even top 500 athletes. Some of these athletes are international but entertained largely American audiences.

The growth of professional football and basketball—and their television audiences—has been phenomenal. Revenues and players' salaries have expanded dramatically. Despite the negative experience of some players' alleged, and in some cases proven, use of performance enhancing drugs, the overall growth and popularity of sports remains quite strong. As a result, many sports have grown at the collegiate level, especially women's sports, after Title IX of the Education Amendments was passed in

1972. Currently, the National Football League, the National Collegiate Athletic Association and others are trying to address the issue of serious concussions in football.

Steel, Automobile and Rubber Industries

The U.S. steel industry had mixed results during the baby boomer decades. For a long time, the booming U.S. steel industry created thousands of good-paying middle class jobs in communities such as Youngstown, Ohio; Gary, Indiana; Pittsburgh, Pennsylvania; and Steubenville, Ohio. The U.S. industry made the best steel in the world at profitable prices. However, several developments led to a serious decline in this powerful industry. U.S. steel plants stayed with the open-hearth furnace process, while the Germans and Japanese switched to more efficient electrical furnaces. Rising labor demands and associated costs also began to put the United States at a disadvantage in the global marketplace. Over time, U.S. steel lost its competitive advantage, and in the 1980s, the collapse began. Some large U.S. steel plants closed down completely. In some communities, it caused serious economic decline and the loss of thousands of good middle class jobs. Some of those communities are still struggling to find viable alternatives for jobs. There is a much smaller recovery occurring now, with specialized mills and products like pipelines for natural gas and oil exploration. U.S. steel's percentage of world steel production remains incredibly low: In 2009, U.S. production was 19 million metric tons, and the world's was over 900 million metric tons.

The U.S. auto industry also has had very mixed results over the baby boomer decades. First, there was almost unbelievable growth: In 1945, 725,000 cars were sold in the United States; by 1950, 8 million had been sold. These cars were purchased by the baby boomers' parents. Initially, the auto industry was fine during the early years of the Baby Boomer Generation. The big three U.S. companies were General Motors, Ford and Chrysler. Family sedans were very popular, industry profits were fine, and many good-paying middle class jobs (with benefits and pensions) resulted.

In the 1970s, the U.S. auto industry's status started to unravel with international competition and high oil and gasoline prices. At first, Japanese imported cars were considered very cheap and poor quality. However, due largely to the U.S. statistician Edward Deming and his quality control principles, the Japanese began to significantly improve the quality and safety of their cars, while maintaining lower prices than U.S. cars. Deming's methods had been rejected by the U.S. auto industry when profits were good and the U.S. cars were still quite popular. Over time, the quality of the Japanese cars outperformed U.S. cars, as rated by Consumer Reports and others. Then the U.S. sales of Japanese cars began to soar, and sales of U.S. cars declined, continuing for several decades before the U.S. auto industry began to significantly improve their cars' quality. Unfortunately, the Great Recession of 2007–2009 seriously affected the auto industry. General Motors and Chrysler needed the help of the federal government and the industry's international partners to emerge healthy again. Concessions were made by the auto companies and workers as well. By 2012, car sales peaked again due to pent up demand and government-aided bankruptcy procedures. Ever since the oil crisis in the late 1970s, the U.S. auto industry—with the federal government's encouragement—has steadily improved gas mileage and reduced its carbon footprint.

The U.S. rubber and tire industry during the Baby Boomer Generation's years has ranged from the peak status of Akron, Ohio, as king of the world's rubber and tire industry to today's restrictions on Chinese imported tires so the U.S. industry can compete for a much smaller share of the world market. During its peak, the U.S. rubber and tire industry's largest four tire companies were headquartered in Akron: Goodyear, B.F. Goodrich, Firestone and General Tire. Thousands of good middle class jobs were created up to the industry's peak around 1970. The history of the U.S. tire industry often parallels that of U.S. steel over the past 60 years.

Energy

The history of the U.S. energy industry is mixed as well. In the 1970s, dependence on foreign oil and gas became a very serious issue as prices soared and gasoline shortages forced consumers to wait in long lines at gas stations. U.S. energy is currently in a large transition, with a much improved outlook for self-sufficiency if environmental issues can be satisfactorily resolved through improved extraction and distribution methods. Hydraulic fracturing methods used to open oil and gas shale deposits are very promising, especially for U.S. natural gas production. This shale gas boom is expected to continue until least 2040 and then taper off some.

Hydrofracking is not without controversy, as there are legitimate environmental concerns about the effects on water and air quality. Small earthquakes in Youngstown,

Ohio, and the Oklahoma City area were directly related to the disposal of hydrofracking wastewater. In other areas of the country, some consumers have experienced minor gas explosions in their sinks from gas in the water supply. The momentum for energy self-sufficiency is so strong that hydrofracking will likely continue, hopefully with government oversight on environmental problems and improved methods. There is likely no risk-free source of energy extraction, storage and distribution (except perhaps solar), but risks must be held to a reasonable minimum.

It is economically exciting to think of an energy-independent United States, as well as one with a reduced carbon footprint. This development may be one of the brightest economic outlooks for the United States. One issue that still needs resolving is the lack of refinery capacity to convert oil to gasoline. There has not been a new major refinery in the United States for over 30 years, and the older refineries (with the exception of one large expansion) have maintenance issues and challenges. Alternate forms of green energy, while increasing over time, are not the dominant sources today. Until then, the oil, natural gas and remaining coal industries must be utilized in the American economic engine, following existing and future environmental regulations.

Global Economy and World Trade

The impact on the United States of a global economy and world trade is a hot topic for many, particularly the many average Americans who lost their jobs and/or businesses as a result.

The United States has always been part of an international economy. But the drastic expansion of the global economy began in the 1970s, with the United States' need for oil produced outside the country, mostly from Saudi Arabia. As a result of a more global economy and cheaper labor costs outside the United States, millions of American jobs were lost in the steel, rubber, textile, automobile and other manufacturing industries.

Consequently, a large trade imbalance started to affect the United States. The imbalance grew with the adoption of the North American Free Trade Agreement (NAFTA), signed in 1994. However, trade increased between Canada, Mexico and the United States as a result.

The trade imbalance worsened after China changed its economy to a manufacturing-based export economy around 2000 and China joined the World Trade Organization (WTO) in 2001. Chinese exports of goods to the United States expanded rapidly.

Many economists consider trade expansion to be a positive trend. U.S. consumers have benefitted by having many consumer goods to choose from at reasonable prices. However, a very dear price was paid as millions of Americans, especially those in manufacturing, lost their jobs and many lost their businesses. Although the federal and state governments provided unemployment insurance, job retraining, food stamps and other assistance, it was not nearly enough.

Most American workers want meaningful jobs with decent wages. Unfortunately, wages have been stagnant for several decades, which has caused additional stress and concern among workers. Displaced workers need job retraining to gain the skills they need to work in today's workforce. Germany's apprenticeship training programs, especially in the trades, are generally better than those in the United States. A joint effort by all levels of government and corporate America is needed to help American workers.

Turning the clock back to the 1950s and 1960s, a period of trade isolationism and large tariff increases, is not likely to help and could result in a trade war, which would hurt the U.S. and world economies. Ben Bernanke, former Chairman of the Federal Reserve, strongly advised against this type of action. After all, one in five American jobs are directly related to total trade. U.S. exports account for about 14.5 million U.S. jobs; imports account for about 23.5 million.

Mechanisms exist for resolving trade disputes, such as NAFTA between the United States, Canada and Mexico. Any of the countries, and individual companies, can file a complaint if they suspect the dumping of cheap goods or currency manipulation. A formal body composed of representatives from the three countries review the complaints and decide whether corrective action is appropriate. A similar mechanism exists between the United States and China: WTO.

Regardless of NAFTA and WTO, even dispute cases with sufficient evidence take time to be resolved. By the time a ruling is handed down, some of the damage is already done.

The good news is that the global economy and world trade have had a positive effect—a reduction in world poverty. Even so, poverty and income inequality remain serious problems in the world and in the United States. Wealth is being distributed disproportionately to the rich.

Because many Americans do not wish to move geographically, some of the solutions to massive job losses must be undertaken at the community level. Drawing new economy businesses and retraining workers would likely help communities. But this is extremely difficult to achieve when one or two major employers shut down in a community and leave many residents unemployed, as exemplified by the steel job losses in Youngstown, Ohio, and Gary, Indiana; textile job losses in the Carolinas and New England; and automobile job losses in Michigan and elsewhere.

A current example is the U.S. coal mining industry, concentrated mostly in West Virginia and Wyoming. Workers who lose their jobs receive some help from the federal and state governments but usually not nearly enough. A more formidable effort by all levels of government and the private sector is needed to help these workers. Large cities, such as Baltimore and Detroit, also need to improve their efforts to help those who have lost their jobs.

The shift in the American economy from a manufacturing economy to an information, services, technology and data-driven economy is leaving some workers and communities behind. Since around 1985, services have been a higher percentage of the gross domestic product (GDP) compared with manufacturing. Some Americans are benefitting from the new economy because their training, education and skills are better suited to it. We must continue to help workers and communities thrive in the new American economy. Because the economy continually changes, American workers face an ongoing serious challenge. The strong research and development infrastructure in the United States will be critical in developing new and rewarding employment and economic opportunities for all Americans.

The Arts

Following in the footsteps of their parents, grandparents and, in some cases, great grandparents, the baby boomers contributed significantly to the nation's arts and museums. In 1910, when the parents of the baby boomers were still young children, their parents funded the creation of a large new museum, which later became the Museum of American History and Technology, in Washington, D.C. As the Greatest Generation and baby boomers aged, they funded major renovations and additions to the Smithsonian Institution. In the 1960s, major renovations were made and new wings were added to the Museum of American History and Technology. In 1976, the baby boomers' parents funded the creation of a large National Air and Space Museum in Washington, D.C.; in 2003, the baby boomers opened an annex, the Steven F. Udvar-Hazy Center, near Dulles Airport in Northern Virginia. Baby boomers' children and grandchildren are now enjoying and learning from these museums. The National Museum of the American Indian was recently built on the National Mall, and the National Museum of African American History and Culture is currently under construction there. The Mall museums draw visitors from all over the nation and the world; often three or four generations can be seen together enjoying and learning from these marvelous museums.

New York City also has wonderful museums that date back to the parents and grandparents of the Greatest Generation and that have been expanded by the baby boomers: The American Museum of Natural History (founded in 1869, with fantastic displays), the Cloisters, the Museum of Modern Art and others. John D. Rockefeller of the Greatest Generation started the Cloisters in 1936, and the baby boomers funded major renovations in 1988 and 1999. Chicago and Boston also have strong museum programs developed across generations. Major contributions to the arts and museums are truly multigenerational accomplishments for the nation.

Entertainment and Media

In addition to the great contributors to a golden age of music who have already been cited, there were thousands more very talented singers and musicians from the Baby Boomer Generation. The U.S. movie and television industries grew as well, with many innovative and high-quality movies and television shows. Major news programs were dominated by Greatest Generation anchors and analysts: Edward R. Murrow, Walter Cronkite, Chet Huntley, David Brinkley and Eric Sevareid. Their replacements, such as Tom Brokaw, Peter Jennings, Diane Sawyer and Dan Rather, are members of the Silent Generation. These news anchors have influenced baby boomers for decades.

The movie industry has had many famous multi-generational actors and actresses, including John Wayne, Elizabeth Taylor, Bette Davis, Katharine Hepburn, Clark Gable, Robert De Niro, Jack Nicholson and Paul Newman. The list also includes Julie Andrews, Meryl Streep, Julia Roberts, Al Pacino, Russell Crowe, Tom Hanks, Leonardo DiCaprio, Tom Cruise, Denzel Washington and Will Smith. Movies continue to be popular among and entertaining to members of all six living generations.

Other Industries

The great U.S. road and bridge network has yielded incredible growth in the use of commercial trucks for moving goods. Retail giants like Walmart, Target, major food chains and major furniture and other industries move their products on the roads, mostly to their stores. Long- and short-haul truckers occupy many important and necessary jobs.

Industries that supported military missions grew rapidly in the 1950s and remain very strong today. President Eisenhower was the first to refer to it as the powerful military–industrial complex. It also supported the development of the modern airline industry. Some of the powerhouse companies are Boeing, Northrop Grumman, United Technologies, General Electric and Raytheon.

The Challenges Ahead

While I am proud to be an American citizen and consider the United States a truly great nation, it still faces several challenges. Readers will undoubtedly have their own list of remaining major challenges for the United States; here is mine:

1. Keep the nation and citizens secure.

2. Reduce poverty.

3. Reduce crime.

4. Reduce illegal drug consumption.

5. Reduce long-term debt at the federal, state, local and individual levels.

6. Improve education opportunities and outcomes for all.

7. Reduce pollution and carbon footprint without large negative effects on the economy.

8. Increase wages and median household incomes.

9. Improve health care and reduce costs.

10. Increase infrastructure maintenance and development.

11. Balance federal, state and local incoming revenues with citizens' desired outcomes.

12. Design and implement policies to address current and future threats to many jobs from accelerated automation, including robotics and even drones.

To address these issues even partially will take unity and passion of purpose, as well as all levels of U.S. government, corporate America and citizens working together. The challenges and even partial solutions are very complex. Some of the above goals overlap, and some conflict with each other. The last two chapters of this book only partially address part of goal 5: Reduce long-term debt at the federal, state, local and individual levels. The list is very challenging, but the United States usually meets such difficult challenges and can continue to do so.

Chapter VIII
The Legacy of the Current and Cumulative Federal Deficit

The federal deficit is perhaps the largest remaining problem that the Baby Boomer Generation has created and not yet solved for American society. The cumulative gross federal debt is $19 trillion and growing rapidly; the per capita amount is over $50,000 for each U.S. citizen. By the end of President Obama's second term, it will be near $20 trillion. Just the interest on this debt eats up a growing amount of the annual federal budget in the United States, and it will be further exacerbated when interest rates begin to rise again. The annual debt has been around $500 billion for the past several years.

Congress' nonpartisan Government Accountability Office (GAO) has recently stated that Medicare, Medicaid and Social Security are not sustainable in their current forms. With the first of the baby boomers reaching the retirement age of 65 in 2011, the financial stress on these entitlement programs is just beginning. Approximately 10,000 baby boomers a day are reaching age 65. By 2029, there will be over 70 million persons over 65. The great challenge is to take care of this rapidly growing number

of senior citizens without bankrupting future generations.

The concepts of publicly held federal debt and total federal outstanding gross debt are a bit confusing to many,
including the author. Based on federal government
budget and debt data from the Office of Management
and Budget (OMB), the Congressional Budget Office
(CBO) and several leading experts on debt, the author's
best understanding is as follows.

The most commonly reported accumulated federal debt
is the federal outstanding gross debt. That amount is currently around $19.3 TRILLION. It consists of three major
components: (1) debt held by the Federal Reserve, (2)
debt held by the public (which includes foreign countries
such as China and Japan) and (3) debt held by government agencies. The largest component is the publicly
held debt, which is currently around $14 TRILLION.

The following graph from the CBO presents the publicly
held federal debt as a percentage of the total U.S. economy or GDP from the nation's beginning. The graph also
includes projected debt to 2050.

The Legacy of the Current and Cumulative Federal Deficit

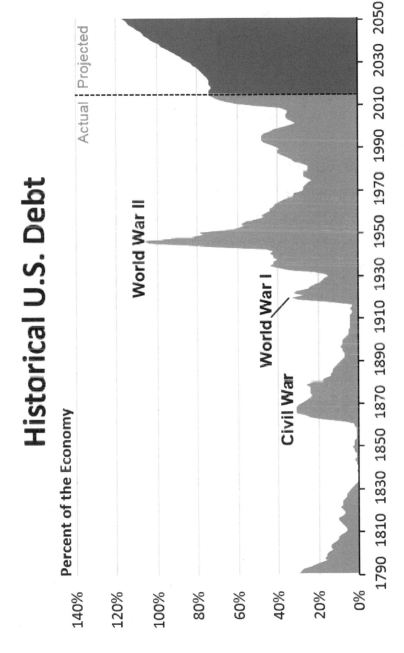

Historical U.S. Debt

Percent of the Economy

Civil War

World War I

World War II

Actual | Projected

140% 120% 100% 80% 60% 40% 20% 0%

1790 1810 1830 1850 1870 1890 1910 1930 1950 1970 1990 2010 2030 2050

Source: CBO 2015 Long-term Budget Outlook

The graph tells an interesting story. It starts with the debt incurred during the Revolutionary War, which was largely paid off by 1814. The next blip up on the graph was after the War of 1812, which was largely paid by 1833. The third upward trend was the result of the Civil War, which was mostly paid by 1890. The fourth upward movement resulted from World War I, which was mostly paid by the mid-1920s. The fifth upward move is associated with the Great Depression. It was not paid down until several decades later. The sixth upward movement is very dramatic and the largest in the nation's history; it is associated with World War II and shows the magnitude of that event. Before the early 1940s, the national debt was never more than 50 percent of GDP. As a result of World War II expenditures, the debt rose to an all-time high of 106 percent of GDP! After the war, the debt was paid down to less than 50 percent of GDP by the early 1960s. It continued to drop until 1980 to around 35 percent of GDP. (Interestingly, the Korean War and the Vietnam War did not increase the debt as a percentage of GDP.)

In 1980, President Ronald Reagan got a major tax reduction program passed by Congress. However, Congress did not pass any significant spending reductions, and the national debt rose to around 65 percent of GDP by the mid-1990s. Under President Clinton, it dropped to around 55 percent of GDP. It started to rise again around 2000 and accelerated further with the terrible September 11 acts of terrorism and the wars in Afghanistan and Iraq. After the 2007–2009 Great Recession and housing and banking crises, the national debt rose dramatically first under President George W. Bush and then even more dramatically under President Barack Obama. Also, medical costs rose rapidly during both of these admin istrations. The national debt is currently around 76 percent. Without major policy changes, it may increase to well over 100 percent by 2030.

James Grant, noted finance expert on the U.S. debt, recently wrote an excellent article in *Time* magazine. He stated, "This much I have learned about debt after 40 years of writing and study: It is better not to incur it. Once it is incurred, it is better to pay it off. America, we have a problem. What awaits us and our children and their children is the unpaid tab of the future."[3]

As if the federal debt isn't scary enough, the federal gross outstanding debt does not include a major item called

---

[3] Grant, James. "The United States of Insolvency: $13,903,107,629,266. Can the Nation Afford This Much Debt?" *Time*. April 25, 2016.

"unfunded liabilities." I believe that this is far more scary. Some social program costs and federal employee pension costs are not included in the federal gross outstanding debt. A rule of thumb by some economists is that the REAL total federal debt is around three times higher than the most often reported federal gross outstanding debt. Using a play on words, I thought it was gross enough already. Real total federal debt by 2040 without major policy changes is forecast to range from $75 TRILLION–$200 TRILLION, which is totally unsustainable. Former Comptroller General David Walker and former OMB Director David Stockman are both in the camp of total unsustainability of the real federal debt and write passionately about the need to start dealing with it now.

The stock market's Dow Jones index fell from 14,200 in October 2007 to 6,500 in March 2009, but it recovered dramatically to approximately 18,000 in early 2015. However, many baby boomers' retirement plans and savings suffered serious damage. Paying for several wars and improving domestic security after the September 11 attacks led to a surge in federal spending during the George W. Bush administration. Unemployment began to peak, and continued bailouts of some of the financial institutions and the American auto industry were instituted by the Barack Obama administration, leading to a much higher surge in federal spending. Some of the especially hard-hit economic areas were Flint, Michigan (which now is experiencing a tragic water safety crisis as well); Youngstown, Ohio; several former textile factory towns from the Carolinas to New England; and other former steel and industrial towns in the Rust Belt of the Midwest.

On the brighter side, the recent rise in the stock market has provided substantial relief to those baby boomers who were invested in the market and saving for retirement. Also, the 7-year slow but steady reduction in unemployment has helped many Americans. Wages have remained stagnant, sometimes for decades, but they are starting to increase, although very slowly. Some baby boomers had to liquidate their stock holdings during the stress period and did not benefit from the recovery. However, many others have experienced additional financial stress as they have become members of the "Sandwich Generation": First, their parents have become quite elderly and often need caretaking. Second, some of the boomers' children are living at home longer due to difficulty in finding jobs; some are also carrying larger debts from college expenses, which continue to rise much more rapidly than any inflation index. Student loan debt has doubled in the past decade and is over $1.3 trillion. This cost must be reduced for students and their families.

Politicians and policy-makers are thus struggling with recovery from the Great Recession and an unsustainable long-term debt at the same time. Any short-term severe austerity measures threaten the recovery, and yet ignoring the long-term debt is also unwise.

As this book is being published, the nation is in the middle of a presidential election season. As promised, this book aims to be nonpartisan. My considerations when evaluating various candidates include, on the personal level, the candidate's pertinent experience, charisma, leadership ability, communication skills, demeanor and behavior. On the policy level, I evaluate the candidates' proposals (and their prospects for passing Congress) on these topics: the economy and employment, taxes, energy, the environment, immigration, national defense and homeland security, federal social programs and education.

I encourage all those eligible to cast their votes based on their own evaluations and beliefs. I am happy to see the big turnouts for the first time among the millennials, as they need to represent their generation. A large voter turnout is good for the nation.

Chapter IX
Baby Boomers' Last Chance to Improve Their Legacy

The U.S. federal government has accumulated deficit numbers that are staggeringly high, growing rapidly and obviously not sustainable. GAO's recent reports and website declare that Medicare, Medicaid, the Affordable Care Act, or Obamacare, and Social Security are unsustainable with the current levels of benefits and revenue sources; the systems will be seriously out of balance by the 2020s. Thus, the impending debt crisis may peak around 2030 and be with us for a long time without solutions. In 2010, President Obama set up the high-ranking, bipartisan National Commission on Fiscal Responsibility and Reform (often called the Simpson Bowles Commission) to study the debt crisis and propose solutions to alleviate it.

The Simpson–Bowles Commission released a comprehensive draft report in December 2010 and a second report in 2013. Highlighting the difficulty of obtaining agreement on potential solutions, the plan outlined in the 2010 report got only 11 of the 14 commission votes necessary for approval. The report recommended a combination of some rather large federal program cuts and some new revenue sources. Both reports' recommendations would involve serious sacrifices by many Americans.

The goal of Simpson–Bowles II is to cut, over a decade, the accumulated publicly held debt to a level of 70 percent of GDP. President Obama's current goal is 73 percent of GDP. We are currently at 76 percent. Without further action, we are headed to well over 80 percent of publicly held debt to GDP. The only time this ratio was higher was after the World War II expenditures, when it reached well over 100 percent. Changes proposed in Simpson–Bowles II include further tax reforms; a chain weighted or shaved consumer price index (CPI) for all federal programs that use the CPI for inflation adjustments, such as Social Security; Medicare premium increases for the wealthy; cuts in farm subsidies; and the reduction of fraud in Medicare and other federal programs such as SNAP. A Simpson–Bowles I recommendation not yet fully acted upon is to raise the cap for Social Security taxes on the wealthy, making it a more progressive tax.

In a 2013 Bloomberg News article by Katherine Burton (based on an interview with Steven Druckenmiller by Bloomberg's Stephanie Ruhle), Druckenmiller said the mushrooming costs of Social Security, Medicare, Medicaid and the Affordable Care Act may have unfunded liabilities as high as $200 trillion in the future. David Walker, the U.S. Comptroller General for 10 years, makes similar claims. Even if they are both estimating too high by a multiple of two, the numbers are still staggering. These are two experts claiming very dire consequences unless politicians, on a bipartisan basis, begin to take the painful necessary steps to prevent incredible economic pain.

It is not obvious how to improve the overall U.S. economy's GDP and reduce unemployment while addressing the unsustainable accumulative deficit. Even professional economists have major differences in opinions, ranging from "the debt is not a problem for another 10 years" to "it is a huge problem already." The serious debt problem will peak around 2025–2030. It won't become easier when more of the baby boomers start expecting Social Security payments and Medicare and Medicaid benefits, where some of the serious sacrifices will have to occur. A sustainable federal budget will have to reduce spending and most likely also increase tax revenues. Although it's a straightforward budget issue, the highly charged debates about *how* to cut spending (thus reducing someone's benefits) and *how* to raise taxes (on almost all individuals and businesses) are incredibly difficult. However, as a great American society, we probably have no better choices. We must realize that we are all in it together and must think not only of ourselves but also of our children, grandchildren and perhaps great grandchildren. It will be somewhat painful and challenging to give up some government-provided benefits and programs. When elected politicians finally address these very serious national problems on a bipartisan basis, which is necessary for success, some significant progress can be made. A balance between achievable revenues and expenditures for the public good needs to be defined and struck. The answers do not likely lie in only austere, drastic cuts or only tax-and-spend alternatives.

I am sure the vast majority of baby boomer–led families are already trying to follow in their Greatest Generation parents' footsteps and leave a sound financial and social environment for their children and grandchildren. We need to mimic that effort on a national level and approach the federal government's accumulated debt with similar dedication and sacrifice. However, baby boomers' ability to contribute will vary greatly. The variation in just income is staggering, from those baby boomers living below the poverty line to successful businesspersons like Bill Gates and Jeff Bezos. To their credit, Gates and his spouse, Melinda; Warren Buffet; Mark Zuckerberg and his spouse, Priscilla Chan; and other philanthropists have started successful initiatives to aid the poor and deliver medical services around the world. Good governance and the private sector's and citizens' work toward common causes create progress.

The American economy is based on a regulated capitalism model that has generally served the nation well. There are exceptions, of course, from the Great Depression to the more recent Great Recession of 2007–2009. The right amount and type of regulation will always remain challenging and debatable. A no-regulation approach would be disastrous environmentally and economically. Over-regulation can also be a very serious problem. For example, there are necessary food safety regulations; without some of them U.S. citizens would get sick and sometimes die from bad food supplies. Which regulations are the most important and most necessary? When low-priority regulations become too expensive and cumbersome, that can be a problem as well.

Our politicians and the American public need to address this very serious issue by governing toward the middle and not solely at the extremes. This will take a *mature*, bipartisanship form of governing, which seems to be escaping us now. After you take into account the extreme right and extreme left, there is 70 percent of us left that also needs representation. Perhaps the silent majority will need to begin speaking again about governing towards the middle for the benefit of most Americans. Since there are mass media representations of the right and left wings blaring each day on television and radio, it makes it more difficult to govern from the middle. While it is good to have all views represented, it would seem desirable to have it somewhat proportionate to the total population's makeup. The silent majority may have to try harder to be represented in this political and governing environment. Former Senator Olympia Snowe, now with her Women's Leadership Institute, has recently made this point in her speeches and television appearances. The nature of politics has always required some degree of compromise. The debt crisis will only get much worse before it hopefully gets better. By 2025, the politicians in power will no longer be able to kick this can down the road: The can will be at least gallon-sized and full of cement, so kicking it will no longer be feasible! Only reasonable solutions will be acceptable then. Hopefully, we can get an earlier start on solutions.

At least we have begun to take baby steps, although not at all smoothly. In January 2013, the 2-year temporary

Social Security payroll tax cut was eliminated, adding some revenue. A small increase in the cap of income taxed for Social Security, an increase in some tax rates and some reductions in deductions for the wealthy are a beginning, but they fail to address the benefit side. In addition to those put forth in the Simpson Bowles reports, other potentially major saving ideas are means testing and raising the eligibility age for federal benefits programs.

There are many ideas for smaller savings. A recent GAO report identified overlapping federal programs that should be considered for consolidation. The author suggests keeping pressure on federal agency administrators to continually improve productivity and cost efficiency without cutting critical services to the American public. It is difficult to suggest the infamous "deliver more for less," but it should be an achievable goal to "deliver the same for less" over time. The reward mechanism for federal agency administrators could be changed from spending 99.99 percent of their appropriated budget to coming in under budget. They could also be allowed to keep a rather small portion of the savings to reward their innovative employees who contributed to the savings. However, the vast majority of the savings should go to the Treasury Department and only be used to pay down the debt directly. Although the author believes that the vast majority of federal workers are productive and devoted, a small percentage of workers are poor performing and should be held more accountable. Also, federal worker travel could be reduced by using new technologies such as Skype and GoToMeeting more frequently. After all, some obvious abuses have occurred in the General Services Administration (GSA) and elsewhere in the past few years.

These are just a few relatively minor suggestions by the author. If an agency like the nonpartisan GAO could gather ideas from thousands of Americans, more small-scale savings could be obtained. They could immediately discard any truly frivolous suggestions. The American people are a great source for good ideas. Let's use social media and even older technologies like email to gather and evaluate some of these ideas.

Perhaps the most difficult challenge will be any cuts in health care and Social Security benefits. Many Americans may not realize that, although they contribute to Social Security and Medicare throughout their career, for each dollar contributed to Medicare, the program spends $3. The rest is funded by general tax revenues and by additions to the debt. Granted, people have contributed substantially to both Social Security and Medicare, but the costs of existing benefits are still too high to sustain, especially around 2025 and beyond. The baby boomers have earned the right to be taken care of, so the proposed cuts can't gut these programs. They need to be streamlined for more efficient delivery. This is undoubtedly an oversimplification of the process. Changes in these programs need to take into account the economic status of those involved: Some truly economically poor baby boomers will be unable to contribute to the immense sacrifices required. It will require a president with vision and charisma, a bipartisan Congress and a public willing to sacrifice for the overall good of American society.

It is sometimes very popular to say "cut, cut, cut" federal, state or local spending without addressing the true value of government services such as defense, national security, Social Security, Medicare, Medicaid, education policies and programs, agricultural and energy research and air traffic controllers. Many of these programs need to be made more cost-efficient.

A major national goal should be to pass on an equal if not better standard of living to Generations X, Y and Z and other future generations. Without some serious fixes to the unsustainable federal budget deficit, Generation X and future generations face, on average, a potentially serious decline in their standard of living compared with the Baby Boomer Generation. The currently high costs of higher education and its potentially declining rewards also do not bode well for the United States' continued greatness as a nation. Education and opportunities for minorities and all U.S. children must be continually improved to reduce economic and social gaps. The nation needs a talented workforce to address the serious problems and challenges mentioned.

Challenges for the current and future U.S. presidents, Congresses and citizens are many and very complex, but that can't be an excuse to avoid addressing the most pressing problems in a bipartisan effort for the common good. One very great challenge is to decide when a war (costly in both human and economic terms) is truly justified. The United States can't afford to be the world's police. When war is truly justified, such as in World War II, then the U.S. public will strongly support the cause from beginning to end.

The election of the United States' first African-American president, Barack Obama, in 2008 was certainly historic and the beginning of Generation X's influence on U.S. leadership. Even though President Obama is a baby boomer, his Generation X voters were influential in his election in 2008 and re-election in 2012. Obviously, the U.S. presidency is an extremely difficult job, especially with the challenge of an economic recovery and a very serious long-term debt. Because many members of Congress are baby boomers, some natural generational differences are involved. This president and Congress must be more bipartisan in addressing the United States' highest priorities.

It is extremely important for the administration, Congress and society in general to maintain and improve the nation's melting pot as we address very serious economic challenges. It is too tempting to fall into the trap of pitting one group of Americans, including a generation, against another. We generally are not served by using a few bad actors to describe an entire group. We need to resist the temptation to pit one group against another, whether it's Wall Street versus Main Street, one race versus another, the rich versus the poor, one religion versus another and one generation versus another. All groups need to work together to find solutions that maintain the enormous strengths of democracy and capitalism and provide as many opportunities for all in our great American society. There will be some natural frictions when we debate different solutions, but we cannot let emotions overcome and divide us. In economic, international and security crises, we always need to unite. In the 2016 election, the millennials will vote in large numbers for the first time, representing their generation's needs. All six living U.S. generations will need representation, and all will need to sacrifice something in a national effort to increase opportunity for all.

Some of these challenges and problems seem overwhelming but with the fixes mentioned above and the undoubtedly great future breakthroughs in research and development, the United States can and will remain a truly great nation of opportunity for all generations. After all, the incredibly positive imprint of their Greatest Generation parents and the rather impressive footprint of the Baby Boomer Generation themselves, as outlined here, can inspire us to complete our legacy on a very positive note. We need to leave our children, grandchildren and hopefully great grandchildren a society full of opportunities, both social and economic, and not just a pile of unsustainable debt.

A 2013 special section in *The Economist*, entitled, "America's Competitiveness: Cheer Up," by Edward McBride, gives a potentially brighter outlook based on several factors. One is that the United States remains the largest spender in the world on research and development. Surely, there will be important breakthroughs to improve the economy. Also, the energy outlook for U.S. oil and gas exploration and output is very bright. Those domestic supplies can last for several, if not many, decades. A significant need for infrastructure development and maintenance will create U.S. jobs when the funding becomes more available, by shifting some funding priorities. After all, a $3.5 trillion to $4.0 trillion annual federal budget can still afford to meet many key priorities. The American government is far from broke financially. When green energy becomes more economical on a mass scale and more routine, there will be many new and good jobs related to that development. The future outlook is not just dire economic scenarios.

In conclusion, I urge those baby boomers who are economically able to accept some very difficult cuts in Social Security, Medicare and Medicaid so that their children and grandchildren do not face a severe economic crisis. However, the cuts must not be ridiculously severe, because the baby boomers have paid their payroll and general income taxes for these programs for 3 or 4 decades and have earned reasonable protections as they age. Because of income and total wealth inequality, not all baby boomers can be expected to contribute more than they already are. According to an analysis by Edward N. Wolff of New York University, the top 1 percent of Americans have 35 percent of the total wealth and the top 20 percent have about 89 percent of the total wealth. Thus, the sacrifices required should probably be concentrated in the top 20 to 25 percent of Americans economically.

One approach would be to means test for federal benefits distributions. It sounds simple but would be complex to measure and monitor. A more progressive distribution of federal benefits would allow the most needy to get the most benefits and the well-off to get fewer benefits. Many of those involved might feel like they contributed and earned the full benefits, but they may be asked by society to sacrifice some of those benefits to help future generations of Americans. The impending deficit is not an easy problem and neither are any potential solutions. The United States' long term economic strength is on the line, and it is critically important to address all potential solutions. Our politicians and government must be honest in convincing the American public of the severity of the long term deficit problem.

It will indeed be a delicate balance to be fair as possible to the Baby Boomer Generation and the post–Baby

Boomer Generations as well. It will take sacrifice by millions of Americans to find just, affordable and sustainable solutions. Even with this great challenge, I believe in the end we will meet it as we have met many others and keep the United States a very strong and powerful nation. All six living generations in our great nation will contribute to the difficult solutions and overcome many potential barriers to growth and opportunity for all.

Bibliography

Altman, Roger C. "The Great Crash of 2008." *Foreign Affairs*. January–February 2009.

Amadeo, Kimberly. Beyond the Great Recession: What Happened and How to Prosper. World Money Watch. 2010.

Bilmes, Linda J., and Joseph E. Stiglitz. "The Ten Trillion Dollar Hangover." *Harper's*. January 2009.

Brokaw, Tom. *The Greatest Generation*. Random House. 1998.

Clark, Don. "Demand Grows for Supercomputers." *The Wall Street Journal*. March 29, 2013.

Conger, Krista. "How Nanotechnology Could Detect and Treat Cancer." Phys.org. May 18, 2016.

ConstitutionFacts.com. "Twenty-Five Landmark Cases in Supreme Court History." Accessed June 15, 2016.

Crittenden, Michael R., and Marshall Eckblad. "Lending Falls at Epic Pace." *The Wall Street Journal*. February 24, 2010.

Dvorak, Petula. "Sandwich Generation Is Feeling the Bite." *The Washington Post*. March 1, 2013.

Farrell, Diana, David Court, Eric Beinhocker, et al. *Talkin' 'Bout My Generation: The Economic Impact of Aging U.S. Baby Boomers*. McKinsey Global Institute. June 2008.

Fox, Justin. "Are We Broke Yet?" *Time*. September 14, 2009.

Friedan, Betty. *The Feminine Mystique*. W.W. Norton & Co. 1963.

Gold, Russell. "Gas Boom Projected to Grow for Decades." *The Wall Street Journal*. February 28, 2013.

Goldstein, Amy. "Alarm Sounded on Social Security." *The Washington Post*. May 13, 2009.

Gorbachev, Mikhail. Perestroika: New Thinking for Our Country and the World. Harper & Row Publishers. 1987.

Grant, James. "The United States of Insolvency: $13,903,107,629,266. Can the Nation Afford This Much Debt?" *Time*. April 25, 2016.

Green, Carl R. Walking on the Moon: The Amazing Apollo 11 Mission. Enslow Publishers. 2012.

Green, Kelley, and Anne Tergerson. "Delayed Retirements Are Boon and Bane for Firms." *The Wall Street Journal.* July 13, 2009.

Hanuschak, George Jr. *Baby Boom Debt Legacy.* Chantilly, Virginia, High School Report. February 28, 2005.

Huntsman, Jon M. Jr., and Joe Lieberman. "Stop Fighting, Start Fixing." *Fortune.* May 1, 2016.

Ignatius, David. "The Baby Boomers' Retirement Bummer." *The Washington Post.* May 7, 2009.

Jurey, Philomena. *A Living History of the 1960s.* Linus Press. 2013.

Kiplinger, Knight. "A Stubborn U.S. Budget." *Kiplinger Newsletter.* April 2010.

McBride, Edward. "America's Competitiveness: Cheer Up." *The Economist.* March 16, 2013.

NASA Spinoff website. "History and Current Spinoffs from U.S. Space Program."

Novak, Jill. "The Six Living Generations." Marketing Teacher Website.

Pearlstein, Steven. "A Defining Moment for American Capitalism." *The Washington Post*. May 27, 2012.

Plumer, Brad. "Back to Made in America?" *The Washington Post*. May 1, 2013.

Rosenthal, Jonathan. "Twilight of the Gods." *The Economist*. May 11, 2013.

Samuelson, Robert J. "Economists Out to Lunch." *The Washington Post*. July 6, 2009.

Samuelson, Robert J. "Let Them Go Bankrupt Soon." *Newsweek*. June 1, 2009.

Saslow, Eli. "Hungering for a New Month to Begin." *The Washington Post*. March 27, 2013.

Schneider, Howard. "Waiting for Recovery? It Could Be Awhile." *The Washington Post*. February 28, 2013.

Shultz, George P., Michael J. Boskin, John F. Cogan, et al. "Principles for Economic Revival." *The Wall Street Journal*. September 16, 2010.

Singer, P.W., and Allan Friedman. *Cybersecurity and Cyberwar*. Oxford Press. 2014.

Smiley, Robert A., and Harold L. Jackson. Chemistry and the Chemical Industry: A Practical Guide for Non-Chemists. CRC Press. 2002.

"Summarizing the New Simpson-Bowles Plan." Fix the Debt. April 23, 2013

U.S. Government Accountability Office (GAO) website. "Data on U.S. Debt—Historic and Current."

Walker, David. "The Deficits Are Coming." *The Wall Street Journal*. September 5, 2009.

Walker, David M. Comeback America: Turning the Country Around and Restoring Fiscal Responsibility. Random House. 2010.

Will, George F. "Recovery Meet Sobriety." *The Washington Post*. June 11, 2009.

Wolff, Edward N. "Changes in Household Wealth in the 1980s and 1990s in the U.S." Edgar Publishing Ltd. November 2012.

Yankelovich, Daniel. Wicked Problems, Workable Solutions: Lessons From a Public Life. Rowman & Littlefield. 2015.

Yergin, Daniel. The Prize: The Epic Quest for Oil, Money & Power. Simon and Schuster. 2008.

Yergin, Daniel. The Quest: Energy, Security, and the Remaking of the Modern World. Penguin Press. 2011.

Zumbrun, Josh. "Baby Boomers Pile on the Debt." The Wall Street Journal. February 13–14, 2016.

Space for Reader Notes

Space for Reader Notes

Space for Reader Notes

The back cover is a picture of the author's immediate family in 1953. It is one of my favorite Greatest Generation to Baby Boomer Generation moments and childhood memories as a baby boomer. The picture includes my father, Mickey; my mother, Flora; my sister, Jean; and me. It was taken at an amusement park in western Pennsylvania at the annual picnic of my father's employer, the East Ohio Gas Co. All his co-workers and their spouses and children attended and had a good time.